LOVE DOES

DISCOVER A SECRETLY INCREDIBLE LIFE
IN AN ORDINARY WORLD

BOB GOFF

THOMAS NELSON
Since 1798

NASHVILLE   DALLAS   MEXICO CITY   RIO DE JANEIRO

Published in Nashville, Tennessee, by Thomas Nelson. Thomas Nelson is a registered trademark of Thomas Nelson, Inc.

Thomas Nelson, Inc., titles may be purchased in bulk for educational, business, fundraising, or sales promotional use. For information, please e-mail SpecialMarkets@ ThomasNelson.com.

The quotation in "Bigger and Better" is taken from C. S. Lewis, *The Weight of Glory* (orig. 1949; New York: HarperOne, 2001), 26.

Library of Congress Control Number: 2012933533

ISBN-13: 978-1-4002-0375-8

Printed in the United States of America

13 14 15 16 RRD 15 14 13 12 11 10

This book is dedicated to
Sweet Maria, Lindsey, Richard, and Adam and the
posse of friends who have changed the way I see Jesus

CONTENTS

CONTENTS

FOREWORD

by Donald Miller

Bob Goff has had a greater impact on my life than any person I've known. And while you'll read stories in this book about adventures both big and small, it isn't bears or witchdoctors or dynamite that got through to me, though I confess Bob's adventures are intoxicating. The reason Bob has impacted my life is because he loves me.

Bob Goff loves people with a force that is natural, and by natural I mean *like nature*, like a waterfall or wind or waves on the ocean. He loves effortlessly, as though love packs annually in snow on a mountain, melting and rushing through him in an infinite loop. There's no explanation for a man who can love this well save God. I think Bob Goff knows God, and I think God's love flows through him.

I'm not alone in these sentiments. There are many around the world who have experienced the same love. What do you do with a man who will get on a plane and fly around the world to attend the wedding of a new acquaintance? What do you do with a man who offices at Tom Sawyer Island at Disneyland because angry lawyers are less likely to yell at him there, and for that matter, what do you do with a lawyer whose business card simply reads *Helper*? What do you do with a man who worked for two years to free a child from a prison in Uganda, all because I met the kid and asked him to? How do you explain the fact that he lumbers, pajama-clad, into his garden every morning to find a rose for his sleeping wife? And then there's the old lady who ran into his jeep, sending his body flying into the street to whom he also sent flowers. There're the DC diplomats, the new acquaintances to whom he daily sent pizza for a week, the Ugandan judiciary that he took to Disneyland, and the refugee camp outside Gulu where he dug wells and delivered pounds and pounds of clothes.

I don't know how to explain Bob's love except to say it is utterly and delightfully devastating. You simply cannot live the same once you know him. He will wreck your American dream and help you find your actual dream. He will wreck your crappy marriage and help you find a love story. To know Bob is to have a façade you've spent your life maintaining beautifully strewn to ruins while, like a friend, he comes alongside you as you rebuild.

Bob has offered to get on a plane on my day of trouble, called exactly when I needed him to, spoke a word of truth when I was being bombarded with lies, given me a family, given me a home, given me a vision for what can happen in a person's life when they are devoted to giving it away.

This book will be troubling for some. We don't like to put hands and feet on love. When love is a theory, it's safe, it's free of risk. But love in the brain changes nothing. Bob believes that love is too beautiful a concept to keep locked up behind a forehead like a prisoner.

Those I've introduced Bob to, and there have been many, find it hard to put into words what is different about him. But the title of this book says it all. Where you and I may want love and feel love and say love, Bob reminds us that love does things. It writes a letter and gets on a plane. It orders pizza and jumps in a lake. It hugs and prays and cries and sings. Much of what we've come to know and believe about love doesn't ring true once you know this man whose *love does*.

What a privilege to introduce you to my friend Bob Goff.

Sincerely,
Donald Miller

LOVE DOES

*I used to think I needed an office to be a lawyer,
but now I know all I need is an island.*

I do all of my best thinking on Tom Sawyer Island at Disneyland. There's a picnic table at the end of a little pier right across from the pirate ship. I suppose most people think this place is just a prop because there are a couple of wooden kegs marked "gunpowder" and some pirate paraphernalia hung over the railings. But it's not just a prop to me; it's my office.

All the times I've gone, I've never seen anyone sitting at my table on my pier or any real pirates on the pirate ship. I guess that makes them my table, my pier, and my pirate ship. Lawyers just decide stuff like that. While I'm willing to share my table and my pirate ship, truth be known, I only want to share it with people who can dream. We all want to have a place where we can dream and escape anything that wraps steel bands around our imagination and creativity. Tom Sawyer Island is a place where I conspire with people, where immense capers have been launched, and where whimsy runs wild. The return address for many of the stories you'll find in this book is, in fact, that pier on Tom Sawyer Island.

What I like the most about Tom Sawyer Island is that it's mine. I'm a good sport about sharing it with other kids and visitors. But the whole thing is mine nonetheless. Something happens when you feel ownership. You no longer act like a spectator or consumer, because you're an owner. Faith is at its best when it's that way too. It's best lived when it's owned.

I have a season's pass to Disneyland and I can take a train there anytime I want. If I want to take a friend, I have an old classic motorcycle with a sidecar, a Harley-Davidson Springer Softail I keep in the garage for special occasions. It's the kind of motorcycle you'd see in a picture under the title "whimsy" in the encyclopedia. It's cool. It's blue and it's loud. I like riding it because I'm fully engaged while getting from here to there. I also like that I can bring a friend along as well. When I pass by people they smile because they've never been in a sidecar, but I can tell they wish they were the passenger. Whimsy is a lot that way—it needs to be fully experienced to be fully known. Whimsy doesn't care if you are the driver or the passenger; all that matters is that you are on your way.

Here's a strange truth I've noticed. Almost everyone knows about Tom Sawyer Island at Disneyland, but most people don't go. Maybe it's because it's surrounded by water and you have to take a raft to get there. But it's really not that tough to do. Lots of people *want* to go. Some people even plan to go. But most forget or just don't get around to it. It's one of those "we'll do that next trip" kinds of places for a lot of people. Tom Sawyer Island is like most people's lives, I think: they never get around to crossing over to it.

Living a life fully engaged and full of whimsy and the kind of things that love does is something most people plan to do, but along the way they just kind of forget. Their dreams become one of those "we'll go there next time" deferrals. The sad thing is, for many there is no "next time" because passing on the chance to cross over is an overall attitude toward life rather than a single decision. They need a change of attitude, not more opportunities.

There are no admission requirements at Tom Sawyer Island. It doesn't matter how tall or short you are, old or young, religious or not. There are no lines on Tom Sawyer Island; it can be whatever you want it to be. You can do countless things there. Most of them involve running and jumping and using your creativity and imagination. It's a place where you can go and just do stuff. In that way, it's a place that mirrors life well—at least the opportunity to do much with our lives.

From my office on Tom Sawyer Island I have a fantastic perch to look around and see how a sea of people live. Tom Sawyer Island isn't a ride. It's not just about distraction or thrills, and it's not the kind of place you go to be entertained either. It has all the potential you bring to it—nothing more, nothing less. To find out just how much that is, all you have to do is show up. You don't need a plan; you just need to be present.

Somewhere in each of us, I believe there's a desire for a place like Tom Sawyer Island, a place where the stuff of imagination, whimsy, and wonder are easier to live out—not just think about or put off until "next time." This is a weighty thing to think about on my island, but I often consider what I'm tempted to call the greatest lie of all time. And that lie can be bound up in two words: *someone else*. On Tom Sawyer Island, I reflect on God, who didn't choose someone else to express His creative presence to the world, who didn't tap the rock star or the popular kid to get things done. He chose you and me. We are the means, the method, the object, and the delivery vehicles. God can use anyone, for sure. If you can shred on a Fender or won "Best Personality," you're not disqualified—it just doesn't make you *more* qualified. You see, God usually chooses ordinary people like us to get things done.

As I sit on my island, it becomes clear that we need to stop plotting the course and instead just land the plane on our plans to make a difference by getting to the "do" part of faith. That's because love is never stationary. In the end, love doesn't just keep thinking about it or keep planning for it. Simply put: love does.

I'M WITH YOU

I used to want to fix people,
but now I just want to be with them.

When I was in high school, I met a guy named Randy. Randy had three things I didn't have: a Triumph motorcycle, a beard, and a girlfriend. It just didn't seem fair. I wanted all three in ascending order. I asked around and found out Randy didn't even go to the high school; he just hung out there. I had heard about guys like that and figured I should keep my distance, so I did. Later, I heard that Randy was a Christian and worked with an outfit called Young Life. I didn't know much about any of that stuff, but it helped explain the beard and made it okay that he was hanging out at the high school, I guess. Randy never offered me a ride on his motorcycle, but he tried to engage me in discussions about Jesus. I kept him at arm's length, but that didn't seem to chill his interest in finding out who I was and what I was about. I figured maybe he didn't know anyone his age, so we eventually became friends.

I was a lousy student and found out I could take a test to get a certificate that was the equivalent to a high school diploma. I couldn't figure out how to sign up for the test, though, which on reflection was a pretty good indicator that I should stay in high school. My plan was to move to Yosemite and spend my days climbing the massive granite cliffs. At six feet four inches and two hundred and twenty pounds, I didn't really have a rock climber's build. I wonder what made me think there was a rock climber in me? When you are in high school, you don't give much thought to what you can't do. For most people, that gets learned later, and for still fewer, gets unlearned for the rest of life.

At the beginning of my junior year, I decided it was time to leave high school and make the move to Yosemite. I had a down vest, two red bandanas, a pair of rock climbing shoes, seventy-five dollars, and a VW Bug. What else did I need? I'd find work in the valley and spend my off-time in the mountains. More out of courtesy than anything, I swung by Randy's house first thing on a Sunday morning to say good-bye and to let him know I was leaving. I knocked on the door and after a long couple of minutes Randy answered. He was groggy and bedheaded—I had obviously woken him.

I gave him the rundown on what I was doing. All the while Randy stood patiently in the doorway trying his best to suppress a puzzled expression.

"You're leaving soon?" he asked when I had finished.

"Yeah, right now, actually," I said as I straightened my back and barreled my chest to show I meant business. "Look, Randy, it's time for me to get out of here. I just came by to thank you for hanging out with me and being a great friend."

Randy kept his earnest and concerned face, but he didn't say a word.

"Oh, hey," I inserted, "will you tell your girlfriend good-bye for me too, you know, when you see her next?" Again, no words from Randy. He had this weird, faraway look on his face like he was looking right through me. He snapped back into our conversation.

"Hey, Bob, would you wait here for a second while I check something out?"

"No sweat, Randy." I had nothing but time now; what did I care?

Randy disappeared for a few minutes into the house while I stood awkwardly on his porch with my hands in my pockets. When he came back to the door, he had a tattered backpack hanging over his shoulder by one frayed strap and a sleeping bag under his other arm. He was focused and direct. All he said was this: "Bob, I'm with you."

Something in his words rang right through me. He didn't lecture me about how I was blowing it and throwing opportunities away by leaving high school. He didn't tell me I was a fool and that my idea would fall off the tracks on the way to the launchpad. He didn't tell me I would surely crater even if I did briefly lift off. He was resolute, unequivocal, and had no agenda. He was with me.

Despite the kind gesture, it was pretty odd to think he wanted to come along.

"Um, sure, I guess," I said halfheartedly. "You sure?"

"Yeah, Bob, I'm in. If you wouldn't mind, what if I caught a ride with you?" Randy stood with a determined look.

"So, let me get this straight. You want to drive to Yosemite with me—right now?"

"Yep, that's right. I can find my way back after we get there and you get settled in."

I'm not sure why I accepted Randy's generous self-invitation. I guess it's because it caught me totally off guard. No one had ever expressed an interest in me like that before.

"Sure . . . ," I stammered as we both stood awkwardly on his stoop. "Uh, I guess we should get going then."

And with that, Randy closed the door to his little house and we walked side by side to my VW Bug. He plopped into the passenger seat and threw his stuff on top of mine on the backseat.

We got to Yosemite before nightfall, and it occurred to me for the first time we had no place to stay. We had a couple of sleeping bags, no tent, and very little money, so we snuck in through the back of a platform tent set up at one of the pay-per-night campsites. We slept toward the back so we could make our escape if an upstanding tent-renter showed up for the night. Fortunately no one came, and the next morning we woke up to a chilly but glorious morning in Yosemite Valley. To the north of us, El Capitan soared three thousand feet straight up like a huge granite soldier. Half Dome dominated the landscape to the east. These were my companions; this was my cathedral. I was in the valleywide living room of my new home. Now it was time to get a job and settle in. I rolled over in my sleeping bag, thinking about how great it was to have Randy with me. I was a little nervous but also excited about my newfound freedom. I was a man now. I felt my chin for any sign of whiskers. Nothing yet, but I shaved anyway, just in case.

Randy and I dusted off the stiffness that comes with tent camping and went to the Camp Curry company cafeteria. I thought I could get a job flipping pancakes in the mornings, which would leave the rest of the day to climb. I finished the job application in front of the manager, handed it to him, and he gave it right back, sternly shaking his head no. He didn't even pretend to be interested, but I was secretly thankful he at least humored me enough to let me apply.

No matter. Undaunted, I went to one of the rock climbing outfitters with a storefront in the valley. I told them I'd do whatever they needed. I was sure that what I lacked in experience I could make up for by what I lacked in maturity or raw intelligence. They said that they didn't have any work for me either and that jobs were tight and almost impossible to get in the valley. I walked out of the store discouraged and looked at Randy, who was leaning against the VW. Rather than feeding my discouragement or saying "I told you so," Randy fed my soul with words of truth and perspective.

"Bob, you can do this thing if you want. You have the stuff it takes to pull it off. These guys don't know what they're missing. Let's try a few more places."

And then, just like he had said the day before on his porch, Randy reiterated his statement: "Either way, Bob, I'm with you." His words gave me tremendous comfort.

I applied at nearly every business in the valley and struck out every time. There were simply no jobs available and no hope of one opening up soon.

The evening approached as the sun sank low in the hills. It

was one of those sunsets displaying the kinds of vibrant colors that would have made a painter's canvas look overambitious. But I was still heartened: this sunset was real, I was in Yosemite, my friend was with me, and I still had a shot at my dream.

Randy and I headed back to the campsite and snuck into the same tent we had commandeered the night before. I didn't sleep well or long as I sorted through my very short list of options. There was no work, I had no money, I was a high school drop-out, Randy snored, and I had to go to the bathroom. That about covered my list of problems from least to greatest.

The next morning came with a crispness that only fueled my anxiety. Randy stirred next to me in his sleeping bag, gave a couple phlegm-filled coughs, and said in a much-too-cheery voice, "Let's go climb some rocks!" We headed to the foot of one of the monolith cliffs and bouldered for a couple of hours, talking trash to each other about who was the better climber. By midday, we headed back to the valley to see if any businesses had miraculously decided to expand their operations overnight. It felt like the shop owners had quietly met somewhere when they learned that I was arriving in the valley and were conspiring against me to dash my dreams. The same rocks I had come to climb were now beginning to look like barricades. I applied at the remaining small storefronts I hadn't tried the day before. Do I even need to waste my breath to tell you what happened?

Randy and I sat on the front bumper of my VW Bug and leaned back against its flimsy and slightly rusted hood that buckled slightly under our weight. The sun was getting low in the valley again, and the granite cliffs I'd hoped to count as neighbors were casting long, dark shadows on the ground, each of the deepening shadows pointing toward the road exiting the valley.

I only had a few bucks left after buying gas, and Randy offered to spring for dinner. As we walked back out to the car after eating, I turned to Randy and said, "You know, Randy, you've been great coming with me and everything, but it looks like I'm striking out. I think what I'll do is head back and finish up high school." After a short pause, Randy said again what had become a comfort to me throughout the trip: "Man, whatever you decide, just know that either way I'm with you, Bob."

Randy had been with me, and I could tell that he was "with me" in spirit as much as with his presence. He was committed to me and he believed in me. I wasn't a project; I was his friend. I wondered if maybe all Christians operated this way. I didn't think so, because most of them I had met up until that time were kind of wimpy and seemed to have more opinions about what or who they were against than who they were for. Without much more discussion, Randy and I exchanged a silent look and a nod, which meant we were done. Without a word spoken, I hopped in the driver's seat of the car, Randy hopped in the passenger seat, and we followed the path cast from the long shadows the day before. I was going back.

We didn't talk much as we left Yosemite Valley or for much of the way home, for that matter. A dream of mine had just checked into hospice, and Randy was sensitive enough to know I needed some margin to think. We drove for five or six quiet hours. Every once in a while, Randy would check on me in his confident and upbeat voice. "Hey, how are you doing, Bob?"

We pulled down some familiar streets and into Randy's driveway. There was another car in the drive next to Randy's that looked like his girlfriend's. She visited often. We walked up to the front door and he opened it. I walked in behind Randy uninvited, but somehow I still felt welcome. On the floor, I noticed a stack of plates and some wrapping paper, a coffeemaker, some glasses. On the couch there was a microwave half in a box. I didn't understand at first. Had Randy just had a birthday? Was it his girlfriend's? A microwave seemed like a weird way to celebrate someone's arrival into the world. I knew Randy wasn't moving because there wouldn't be wrapping paper. Then, from around the corner, the other half of this couple bounded out and threw her arms around Randy. "Welcome home, honey." Then the nickel dropped.

I felt both sick and choked up in an instant. I realized that these were wedding presents on the floor. Randy and his girl-friend had just gotten married. When I had knocked on Randy's door on that Sunday morning, Randy didn't see just a high school kid who had disrupted the beginning of his marriage. He saw a kid who was about to jump the tracks. Instead of spending the early days of his marriage with his bride, he spent it with me, sneaking into the back of a tent.

Why? It was because Randy loved me. He saw the need and he did something about it. He didn't just *say* he was for me or with me. He was *actually* present with me.

What I learned from Randy changed my view permanently about what it meant to have a friendship with Jesus. I learned that faith isn't about knowing all of the right stuff or obeying a list of rules. It's something more, something more costly because it involves being present and making a sacrifice. Perhaps that's why Jesus is sometimes called Immanuel—"God with us." I think that's what God had in mind, for Jesus to be present, to just be with us. It's also what He has in mind for us when it comes to other people.

The world can make you think that love can be picked up at a garage sale or enveloped in a Hallmark card. But the kind of love that God created and demonstrated is a costly one because it involves sacrifice and presence. It's a love that operates more like a sign language than being spoken outright. What I learned from Randy about the brand of love Jesus offers is that it's more about presence than undertaking a project. It's a brand of love that doesn't just think about good things, or agree with them, or talk about them. What I learned from Randy reinforced the simple truth that continues to weave itself into the tapestry of every great story:

Love does.

....

CHAPTER 2

SNIPER FIRE

I used to think I had to act a certain way to follow God,
but now I know God doesn't want us to be typical.

heard about Jesus for the first time when I was in high school
from a guy named Doug, who I used to shoot BB guns with.
We would go out in the woods by a reservoir and shoot at cans
and old car fenders. Neither of us was a very good shot and we
rarely hit what we aimed for, so we just called whatever we hit the
target. There are a lot of people who still do that. Being in the
woods and armed makes a fifteen-year-old feel like he has chest
hair. The prospect of losing an eye also kept us coming back. It's
not necessarily a guy thing—well, actually, yes. It's a guy thing.

One day, Doug's BB gun broke and he got a pellet gun. I

wanted to have a pellet gun too, but I couldn't find someone to hook me up with one, so I kept using my old gun I got when I was eight years old. There was a big difference between Doug's legit pellet gun and my crummy BB gun. My gun didn't shoot very far or very well. After it was cocked once, it could almost shoot across the room. That is, unless a fan was on, then only about half that distance. It did have a slot where you could put a couple of drops of oil that would turn into a little puff of blue smoke when you pulled the trigger. Despite this fun little feature, mine was no match for Doug's gun, and we both knew it. Doug's pellet gun shot like a real gun too. He could pump it up what seemed like an unlimited number of times, and we imagined it could pierce steel. He put a huge scope on the barrel and then put camouflage on the gun, mostly made of old socks painted green and some weeds. It was an awesome piece of firepower compared to my Daisy BB gun, even though mine had blue smoke and his didn't. I thought I'd save up for a pellet gun like Doug's and maybe a rifle rack too. Yes, definitely a rifle rack.

One lazy afternoon, Doug and I were walking side by side along a trail in the woods. I was looking for new cans to shoot or ones to finish off we'd only wounded the week before. Suddenly I noticed Doug wasn't at my side any longer. I looked to the left and right, but Doug was nowhere to be found. When I looked behind me, however, I saw the muzzle of Doug's pellet gun pointing at me from behind a tree, half a green sock hanging from the scope, which was up to his eye. I had become the next tin can, and I did what any hardened gunslinger would do—I ran. As I ran, I cocked my Daisy BB gun with the blue smoke and just over the rise in the hill I turned to defend myself. But before I could get a round off, Doug pulled his trigger and shot me right in the belly.

Doug must have pumped up his gun twenty times or more, because I fell to my knees, looked down, and there was a hole and some blood where the pellet went through my shirt and inside of me. We were both pretty surprised and wonderfully amazed at the same time. We had just become one of those stories you hear about. Doug prayed for me and told me not to walk toward the light. I told Doug he could have my bicycle if I didn't make it. We put gum and leaves over the hole to stop the bleeding and made our way back to Doug's bedroom to get some tweezers and get the pellet out. We splashed some Scope mouthwash on the hole to clean it, then dug in with the tweezers and got the pellet. He awarded me a purple heart, I gave him a sniper medal, and we vowed to go back and shoot at each other as often as we could.

I liked how Doug did life. He was full of adventure and always had some wonderful mischief in mind. Sitting on the edge of Doug's bed laughing about the day, Doug began telling me the story about another man of adventure named Jesus, who lived a long time ago. Like Doug, Jesus wasn't a religious guy. To me, Jesus sounded like an ordinary guy who was utterly amazing. He helped people. He figured out what they really needed and tried to point them toward that. He healed people who were hurting. He spent time with the kinds of people most of us spend our lives avoiding. It didn't seem to matter to Jesus who these people were because He was all about engagement. That's one of the things I saw in Doug. I liked that Doug could be friends with Jesus and still shoot pellet guns. I didn't think that was allowed, but apparently it was.

I don't have one of the harrowing stories you sometimes hear when someone describes his initial encounter with Jesus. I wasn't on drugs, I hadn't committed any felonies, and I hadn't been in jail. I hadn't had much exposure to religion, and what I did know, I didn't particularly understand. There was something about Communion and something about Sunday school, and whatever the question was, Jesus was supposed to be the answer. There was also something about studying the Bible with a bunch of guys on Wednesdays, which sounded weird because I thought you were supposed to read it and do what it said, not just study it. Maybe there was a workbook that went with it. All I knew of faith were fragments and shards of various traditions, but I hadn't ever heard the whole story about who Jesus was and what He wanted the world to know about Him. Despite my lack of prior knowledge, when my sniper friend Doug told me the whole story, it made a lot of sense.

I think it was more about what I saw in Doug than what he had to say to me. In fact, until we were in his room in post-op, we hadn't talked about Jesus much at all. Still, I knew Doug had something I wanted. I never wanted religion. I didn't understand it and didn't particularly want to either. To be honest, I thought being religious was for wimpy guys who didn't get into mischief. Though Doug wasn't a good shot (or he was a great one, depending on how you look at it), he wasn't a wimp and he seemed to know a person—a real, living God who liked him and even loved him even though Doug was as screwed up as I was. Because of Doug, I believed in this God, and I wanted to know Him too. I believed that Jesus wasn't just so much blue smoke to make religion seem like the real thing. He *was* the real thing, and He had a lot of firepower.

I'm in my fifties now and I don't run around in the woods playing with BB guns. That's way too tame. I have a playful spirit, but I'm also a lawyer and have ties and suit jackets in the same closet that holds my now-rusty BB gun. At times I'm struck by how strange it is that the same person who has gone through so many life changes over the years can believe in this God who is still the same because He never changes. And it's even stranger because I have a legal mind and I spend my time proving things for a living. It's very hard to prove God, yet I still go on believing. I have an overwhelming sense of gratitude as I get older because I can see, both through the good times and the bad times, that God has been with me.

Because I'm a lawyer and a follower of Jesus I'm occasionally asked by people about my religion. I'm not always sure what they hope to learn from me, and the first thing I tell them is that they probably shouldn't be talking to me. I don't validate my faith with a church attendance scorecard. I think of church as a vibrant community of people consisting of two or more of varied backgrounds gathering around Jesus. Sometimes they are at a place that might have a steeple or auditorium seating. But it's just as likely that church happens elsewhere, like coffee shops or on the edge of a glacier or in the bush in Uganda. All of these places work just fine, I suppose. When it's a matter of the heart, the place doesn't matter. For me, it's Jesus plus nothing—not even a building.

When my friends ask about my faith, I tell them that a long time ago my friend Doug told me about Jesus and said I could know Him. I didn't start believing in Jesus just because Doug had shot me. But I've never stopped believing in Him even though I've caught some sniper fire from some religious people since then. There's a passage in the Bible that says people who haven't met Jesus are going to think the people who have met Jesus are crazy. I get that look sometimes, and it's usually from people who don't have a lot of creativity or haven't experienced whimsy or haven't played with BB guns or been shot once or twice. The people who slowly became typical have the greatest problem wrapping their minds around a dynamic friendship with an invisible, alive God.

There's nothing wrong with being typical, I guess, but there is nothing fundamentally right about it either. I've never read in Genesis that God created "typical" and called it good. Instead, I think men who were bored made up *typical* and called it, if not good, at least acceptable. People who follow Jesus, though, are no longer typical—God is constantly inviting them into a life that moves away from typical. Even if they have normal jobs, live in normal houses, and drive normal cars, they're just not the same anymore.

The ones Jesus first picked to follow Him started out typical, to be sure. They were unschooled and ordinary. Fishermen, businesspeople, blind people, loose women, rip-offs, and vagrants. They were people who were lousy shots like me and Doug, folks who had been injured in life and patched together with gum and leaves and grace. But like my BB gun, what Christ-followers lack in velocity, they make up for in intensity. They are people who have experienced an intensely intimate friendship with Jesus and move forward with an intensity to parallel that experience.

Jesus lets us be real with our life and our faith. Maybe my BB gun doesn't shoot as far as the next guy's. That used to matter to me, but it doesn't matter to me anymore. What Jesus said we could do is leave typical behind. We could leave all of the comparisons and all of the trappings and all of the pretending of religion. Jesus told the people He was with that it's not enough to just look like you love God. He said we'd know the extent of our love for God by how well we loved people.

Doug and I are still friends. I send him text messages once in a while to see how he's doing and to find out if he's shot anyone lately. I'm not that great at spelling and thankfully my phone autocorrects the words I type for me. What I've noticed, though, is that almost every time I type in the word love, it gets changed to the word live. It's kind of a reminder to me of one of the things I learned from Doug about following Jesus. I learned that fully loving and fully living are not only synonymous but the kind of life that Jesus invited us to be part of. And because of that, our lives don't need to be just puffs of blue smoke anymore.

....

CHAPTER 3

RYAN IN LOVE

I used to think being loved was the greatest thing to think about, but now I know love is never satisfied just thinking about it.

We have a house down by the water, and there's a little grass path where couples hold hands and walk along the bay front. My wife and I sit on the back porch and hold hands a lot too as we watch the couples meander by. We're close enough to the water that they wave to us, and we wave back, a nostalgic snippet from another time where people waved to each other during slow walks. This is how I met Ryan.

One day, Ryan came walking down the path all alone. Ryan waved to us and we waved back like we did to everyone. But instead of moving on, Ryan just stood there on the path, waving and not moving. Because he kept waving, we kept waving. It was a little awkward, honestly. I wondered if perhaps this young man wanted to talk, so to break the tension, I made the short walk from the porch to the path to say hello.

"Hi there, how's it going?" I said, reaching out to shake his hand and give him a break from all the waving.

"Hi, I'm Ryan and I'm in love," he said confidently. Ryan had that glazed-over look that smitten guys get.

"Well, Ryan, that's just great! Congratulations."

"No, no . . . that's not why I came," Ryan stammered. "What I wanted to say is that I walk by your house all the time . . . and I have this girlfriend, you see . . . and . . ." He paused. "I want to know if it would be okay . . ." He paused again. ". . . if I asked my girlfriend to marry me in your backyard?" He talked like he had been holding his breath for quite some time. I was taken aback by this love-glazed kid who would approach a complete stranger and ask to use his house to stage a great caper. But that's the way it is when you are in love, isn't it? All he knew was that he wanted the girl and was going to do whatever it took to get her.

"Ryan, that sounds like a fantastic idea!" I said, laughing.

"Really?" Ryan answered. I guess he had expected an instant no or a gentler "I'll think about it."

"Sure! Go get your girl and let's get you two engaged!" With that, Ryan went half skipping, half floating down the grassy path. I think his feet hit the path about every twenty feet or so. He was being strategic; he was being audacious; he knew what he was going to do. He was going to get his girl.

A few days later, we were sitting on the back porch again. Couples were walking down the path holding hands. We would wave to them and they would wave to us. Then came an animated figure bouncing and waving happily with both arms. It didn't take long for me to figure out that it was Ryan, and I walked down to the path to greet him.

"Hi!" Ryan yelped with his wonderfully goofy, glazed-over, *I'm-in-love* grin.

"Hi, Ryan, what can I do for you?"

"Well, you know how I am going to propose in your back-yard?" Yes, I remembered that. "I was wondering if you think it would be possible for us . . ." He did another Ryan pause, so I knew whatever followed would be a whopper. ". . . to have dinner on your back porch before I pop the question?"

I bit my tongue to keep from laughing out loud. I'd never even met Ryan before that week, and now he was asking if he could have a marriage proposal and dinner on my back porch? *This kid has it bad!* After a short pause, I shot back to young Ryan, "What the heck, of course you can have dinner on my porch, Ryan! That's a great idea! What can I make for you?"

I don't think he heard the question because off went Ryan, down the path. He seemed to be levitating—he may have touched down on the grass once or twice over the next hundred yards. Ryan was another step closer to the prize. He was all in. He was all about doing and not just dreaming. He was going to get the girl.

By now, I found myself looking forward to my afternoon encounters with young Ryan. It reminded me how fun it was to be young and in love. I even started coming home early from work to sit on the back porch waiting for him, checking my watch every five minutes or so, wondering when he would come bouncing down the path with another outlandish request for a total stranger. And sure enough, Ryan came bounding down the path again, so I went down to greet him.

"Hi, Bob. Hey, I was thinking . . ." And then the pregnant pause. "Would it be possible for me to have some friends of mine serve us when we are having dinner on your porch?"

"You bet," I shot back, laughing. I was already this far in with Ryan; what could it hurt to have a few of his friends over? "What a great idea. How many would it take to serve you two dinner?"

Ryan looked up with a Cheshire cat grin and sheepishly said, "Twenty?" *Did he just say he wanted twenty people inside my house to be his servers?* I was wonderfully stunned by the consistently audacious, almost vertical trajectory of Ryan's plans. He wanted twenty people to serve a dinner for two? Now that's service. But when loves does, love does it *big*.

"What a great idea, Ryan! Twenty it is!" I said without hesitation. Ryan bounced away down the bay front. I could tell that his head was ready to explode with anticipation. He had the vision, he had the plan, he had the place, and he had the staff. He was trigger-locked on the goal, and he was going to get that girl.

A few days later, I was at my post. Almost on cue, Ryan came galloping down the path.

"Ryan, how are the plans coming?"

"Well," he said, "I was actually wondering if it would be okay if after dinner, and after my friends leave, you could put some speakers on the porch and maybe we could dance a bit?"

Of course you want to dance on a stranger's porch. "Speakers it is," I told him. "Anything else?" I was trying to get all the possibilities out of him now.

"Well, I think that about covers it for now. I'll ask her to marry me after we dance for a bit."

"Great idea," I said to Ryan. "Go get that girl!" Ryan skipped off.

A day or two passed with no Ryan sightings. I almost felt a low-grade depression sinking in on me. Was the planning over? Were there no more whimsical and outrageous ideas from Ryan as he planned his caper? Was the mischief done? I sat on my porch, reflecting on how contagious Ryan's brand of love was. And then, almost on cue, Ryan came running down the pathway again.

At this point, Ryan was a regular and he bounded across the lawn and up to the porch without hesitation. He was pretty winded, actually, leaning over with his hands on his knees trying to catch his breath. I wondered if I should give him a paper bag to breathe into. After a few long moments, Ryan straightened up. There was a pause while our stares met. I had learned that a pause by Ryan meant there was another whopper of an idea brewing in his head.

"Hey, Ryan, what's up? It's great to see you. How are the plans coming?"

"Do you . . ." He exhaled. ". . . have . . ." He inhaled. ". . . a boat?"

"A boat?!" I was belly-laughing as I asked him to repeat what I thought he'd just said.

"Yeah, do you have a boat?" Ryan asked more confidently as he straightened a bit.

"Well, actually, Ryan, I do!" I said with half enthusiasm and half awe at Ryan's love-induced, audacious bender. He had that glazed look again as he looked me squarely in the eyes.

"Well, can I borrow it?"

Ryan was out of control. He had no idea what an outrageous thing he was asking. But you see, to Ryan, I wasn't a total stranger—no one was. To him, the whole world was full of coconspirators when it came to winning over his love. He was completely unaware of and unimpeded by what was proper, what was acceptable, and what was conventional. Nothing was going to get in the way of what he decided he was going to do.

"Okay, Ryan. The boat's yours!" I said. "I'll take you and your girlfriend out on my boat after dinner at my house, after your twenty friends finish serving you, and after you dance together on my porch. You can pop the question to your girl up on the front deck of my boat."

Ryan floated away once again, clueless of the beautiful ridiculousness this girl was bringing out of him. Ryan was a study in focus, tenacity, and abandon. He was all gas and no brake.

What Ryan didn't realize is that I decided to one-up him. Why should he have all the fun? That night, I called the Coast Guard and told them about Ryan's elaborate plan and his glazed-over enthusiasm for his girl, which had swept him into a state of unparalleled whimsy. Ryan's enthusiasm was contagious, and pretty soon the guy on the other end of the phone had caught the bug too. The Coast Guard officer and I hatched a plan of our own.

When the big night came, everything was in place. The night was balmy, the air was clear, and I think the stars even came out a few minutes early to see Ryan's elaborate scheme unfold.

Ryan and his girl came walking down the path. When they got to the white Nantucket house on the bay, he led her up the stairs and across the lawn toward a candlelit table on the porch.

"Ryan, what are we doing? Is this okay? Whose house is this?" she whispered as she held his arm a little tighter. Ryan pulled out her chair and said this was for her as he sat her down.

The service at dinner by the twenty servers was impeccable, and the after-dinner dance was endearing as these two stood with arms around each other, slowly moving together on the porch. As they danced, they twirled and talked quietly. By now, evening had fully set in and the lights of the city mixed with the stars were starting to dominate the skyline. It was as if the early appearing stars had gone home and invited all of their friends, telling them, "You have *got* to see this."

The evening was coming to its natural end, and Ryan took his girl by the hand and they headed back to the path. I've always wondered what was going through her head during all this. I hope it all felt like a dream.

As they got closer to the dock behind the house, Ryan gripped her hand, turned, and took her toward a boat that was tied to the end.

"Ryan, *what are we doing?*" she half demanded.

"C'mon," is all he had to say as they came onto my boat. I was at the helm and they made their way to the bow. With the stars out in full view, we slowly motored out into the bay. After a short time, we approached the spot where Ryan and I agreed I would stop the boat so he could pop the question. In a total coup de grâce, Ryan had fifty more of his friends on the shore to spell out "Will you marry me?" with candles—just in case he got tongue-tied or overwhelmed in the intensity and whimsy of the moment. With their flickering sign as his backdrop, Ryan got on one knee.

"Will . . ." He exhaled. ". . . you . . ." He inhaled. ". . . marry . . ." He paused. ". . . me?"

There was a gasp followed by an immediate and enthusiastic yes.

In this, the most special moment of their lives, neither Ryan nor his bride-to-be noticed that the Coast Guard had pulled in behind us with their firefighting boat, just as the officer and I had planned. I gave the thumbs-up—the sign that she said yes—and he shot off every water cannon he had on the entire rig! It was a scene that belonged in New York Harbor on the Fourth of July with the Statue of Liberty in the background. But it wasn't happening there, it was happening for Ryan because that's the way love rolls; it multiplies. Ryan and his bride-to-be let the mist from the water cannons settle over them like a thousand small kisses.

Ryan's love was audacious. It was whimsical. It was strategic. Most of all, it was contagious. Watching Ryan lose himself in love reminded me that being "engaged" isn't just an event that happens when a guy gets on one knee and puts a ring on his true love's finger. Being engaged is a way of doing life, a way of living and loving. It's about going to extremes and expressing the bright hope that life offers us, a hope that makes us brave and expels darkness with light. That's what I want my life to be all about—full of abandon, whimsy, and in love. I want to be engaged to life and with life.

I enjoy those parts of the Bible where Jesus talks about how much He loves His bride. It makes me wonder if the trees and mountains and rivers are things He planned in advance, knowing they would wow us. I wonder if God returned over and over to this world He placed us in thinking what He had created was good, but it could be even better, even grander. I wonder if He thought each foggy morning, each soft rain, each field of wildflowers would be a quiet and audacious way to demonstrate His tremendous love for us.

I don't know if God was a little bit like Ryan when He created everything, or if Ryan was a little bit like God. But what I do know is that Ryan's audacious love is some of the best evidence I've found of the kind of love Jesus talked about, a love that never grows tired or is completely finished finding ways to fully express itself.

CHAPTER 4

THE REACH

I used to be afraid of failing at something that really mattered to me, but now I'm more afraid of succeeding at things that don't matter.

My first real job was at Lehr's Greenhouse Restaurant. It was a fantastic glass building designed to look like an arboretum. It was the Crystal Cathedral of fine dining. Each table was set inside its own wonderfully ornate, white gazebo. And there were dozens of them. The crystal was perfect, the china was delicate, and the waiters were coiffed and formal in their black tuxedos, cummerbunds, and bowties. When I applied to work at Lehr's, I imagined how great I would look in a tux. How I would memorize the menu and make every prom date or business dinner flawless. I also imagined myself counting my pile of money from generous tips.

In order to become a waiter at Lehr's Greenhouse, I had to start as a busboy and work my way up. I did pretty well, I guess, but then again, how can you screw up collecting dirty dishes? It was hard work, but the thought of being a waiter someday made it all worth it. As a busboy, I learned that tables enveloped in white gazebos, while creating a stunning atmosphere, make for some tight and hard-to-maneuver situations. By the time I got to the tables to pick up dishes, everyone would be gone, and I wondered how the waiters navigated that reach. On my one-year anniversary, the maître d' pulled me aside and said I could buy my tuxedo and become a waiter. I was at the tuxedo shop the next morning as soon as it opened.

When opening night came for me and I had my first shift as a waiter, I was so excited I could barely eat. I sprinted out from my small apartment and grabbed some quick Mexican food around the corner because they wouldn't let us eat the food at the restaurant. I rushed back and slipped on my tuxedo for the first time since trying it on in the store. The tuxedo was expensive, but I knew I'd earn enough in tips over the next month or two to pay for it. I had put down half of the money when I bought it and had agreed to pay off the rest in payments from my new waiter job. I intentionally lingered around the apartment complex where I lived just long enough for everyone living near me to see that I indeed had a tuxedo with a ruffled shirt. I left it to their imagination to figure out just how special I was. I hopped into my thrashed VW Bug, drove to the restaurant, and parked around the corner to make sure no one saw me pull up in a VW. I wanted to have that 007, *My-other-car-is-an-Aston-Martin* look.

The night was cloudless. You could see the stars through the glass ceiling. Cinderella wouldn't have been out of place pulling up in her carriage. There were twinkle lights on all of the gaze-bos. It was like Christmas in July. The whole restaurant had a new feel to me, like I'd been an understudy in a play and now was walking out on the big stage as the lead. The maître d' escorted my first guests to one of the elegant gazebos in my zone. It looked like a wealthy doctor and his business guests. They were each starched and tidy and each guy actually looked like he could be the surgeon general. The women looked like they had stepped off of the cover of *Vogue*. The women sat down as the gentlemen slid in their chairs. As soon as the men were settled, I put napkins in everyone's laps and gave them the speech I had rehearsed a dozen times in my bathroom mirror while my toothpaste and deodorant listened. I told them about the many incredible choices they had that evening for what would cer-tainly be the best food, best service, and most remarkable dining experience of their lives. In a word, I promised that the evening would be flawless.

I placed their orders and after a short time came back to the gazebo with the steaming plates. All seemed to be going well, until the unthinkable happened. As I was making the big reach across the wide table, I felt this massive grumbling somewhere south of my stomach, down as deep as one could imagine. There was no time to react. At the pinnacle of my full extension across the table with a plate of prime rib, out came the most impressive and lengthy gassing you can ever imagine. I hardly had time to regret the Mexican food I'd eaten earlier. This was terrible in its own right. But what was more remarkable is that it went on for-ever. I could have sounded out the alphabet if I could have gotten my hands back there, and no amount of butt tightening would put an end to it.

As I finished my episode, looks of absolute shock from my guests came into focus. I think I heard a woman scream. I'd certainly caught the attention of the surrounding tables. A hushed silence descended on us all and I just stood there, paralyzed, holding the prime rib high over the table. I didn't know what to say, and I was afraid that any movement might set off an aftershock. Finally, one of the men got up, threw the napkin I had placed in his lap on the table, and walked straight to the maître d'. With punishing accuracy I saw him describe what just went down, acting out my full extension as he stood on one foot and leaned over across an imaginary table. The sounds he tried to recount lacked a certain base tone and texture, but overall I think he got the general idea and duration right.

I was fired on the spot. No kidding. With my cummerbund in one hand and bowtie in the other, I walked back to my VW Bug with my head hung low. I sat in the front seat, took a deep breath, and wondered what I was supposed to feel at a time like this. On one hand, I'd just destroyed a year's worth of work. I'd earned that waiter spot playing in the minor leagues, busing tables, and when I finally stepped up to the plate in the major leagues, I swung as hard as I could and hit the umpire in the back of the head. I don't know how I could have messed up any worse, to be honest. Yet on the other hand, I had a story for the ages, a story I could someday tell my kids when they thought they had made a big mistake.

I took in another deep breath and felt this huge grin spreading across my face. The grin was almost happening to me rather than me making it happen. As I drove home, I recounted the events from the last hour or two. I thought about my now-useless tux, the guests, the order, the infamous extension, the gasps, the screams, the firing. I can't lie. I knew even then that it had indeed been an amazing, if not flawless night.

My grandmother, Grandma Mary, used to tell me, "You're nothing until you've been fired once or twice." She didn't give any disclaimers for *how* you got fired, so I assumed her adage still applied to me. For the next six months, I made payments on that tux until I dropped it off at Goodwill and I never tried my hand as a waiter again.

The thing I love about God is He intentionally guides people into failure. He made us be born as little kids who can't walk or talk or even use a bathroom correctly. We have to be taught everything. All that learning takes time, and He made us so we are dependent on Him, our parents, and each other. The whole thing is designed so we try again and again until we finally get it right. And the whole time He is endlessly patient.

I love those passages in Scripture where Jesus teaches the disciples something, saying, "I want to teach you to think differently about life." They walked with Him for years, and some of them didn't learn everything they needed to know until after He'd gone back to heaven. Yet, even though they were slow to learn, they still referred to themselves as His beloved. Failure is just part of the process, and it's not just okay; it's better than okay. God doesn't want failure to shut us down. God didn't make it a three-strikes-and-you're-out sort of thing. It's more about how God helps us dust ourselves off so that we can swing for the fences again. And all of this without keeping a meticulous record of our screw-ups.

I found another job eventually, and eventually I lost that one too. But I lost it because I chose to that time, not because I was fired. Finding things and losing things is what the Bible is all about. God even seemed to encourage it. He talked about losing your job, or even your life, if you want to find it. He talked about losing your status to find real power. He shows that Jesus comes looking for us because people, like sheep, have a knack for getting lost. And when He finds us, we usually aren't dressed in a tux.

Things that go wrong can shape us or scar us. I've had some things go well in my life and some things not go so well, just like you. More have gone well than have gone poorly, but I'm not trying to keep score because I have a different way I measure those things now. God finds us in our failures and our successes, and He says that while we used to think one way about things, now He wants us to think another way about those same things. And for me, I've realized that I used to be afraid of failing at the things that really mattered to me, but now I'm more afraid of succeeding at things that don't matter.

···

CHAPTER 5

THE REARVIEW MIRROR

I used to think I could shape the circumstances around me,
but now I know Jesus uses circumstances to shape me.

A fter high school, I went to Humboldt State University because I wanted to be a forest ranger. Actually, I took one of those aptitude tests in high school and slanted all of the answers so the school would report to my parents that if ever anyone was born to be a forest ranger, it was me. What I anticipated most about being a forest ranger is that you live in the woods, you get a green truck, you get a badge, and, to top it all off, you get a hat with a wide brim. After reading the test results I had rigged, my parents had to agree that I was meant to be a forest ranger, and my mom took me to the mountains where the forest rangers live.

Where are the girls? I thought. This was the first indication that my research had perhaps been flawed.

Forest rangers didn't live in the woods the way I had envisioned either. They lived in green concrete dormitories with cots lined up in rows under fluorescent lights. Their greatest adventure, it seemed, was giving tickets to people parked in the wrong places. They played cards a lot and ate TV dinners. I had envisioned something a bit woodsier and manly, I suppose. Guns, moose heads, snowshoes leaning up against a large stone fireplace, a pile of beef jerky on the table . . . something along those lines. What I learned is that most forestry majors at the university go to work for forest products companies like Georgia Pacific or Weyerhaeuser and manage the cutting down of the forests to make paper or wrappers or those sorts of things. I was discouraged, but it was too late to change schools, so I went to Humboldt as a forestry major.

Shortly into my first year at Humboldt, disenchanted at the lack of girls and the business of harvesting forests in general, I decided it was time to make a change, move to San Diego, enroll at the university, and take up surfing. There would certainly be a future for me in that. What made even more sense to me is that my high school sweetheart, Kathy, was going to UCLA and I could be near her. What I didn't count on, however, was getting my first "Dear Bob" letter in short order.

In her brief letter, Kathy said that after arriving at UCLA she had become "romantically involved with her big brother."

"She's involved with her *big brother*?" I gasped as the limp paper dangled in my hand. "Isn't that against the law or something? Besides, I didn't even know Kathy had a big brother. What's his name, anyway?"

What I later learned is that Kathy had joined a sorority and that a "big brother" was Greek-speak for a guy from a fraternity the sorority sisters pair up with. I was so hurt—I almost wished for the other version I initially understood to salvage my ego. I vowed never to love again. I also vowed never to join a fraternity or be part of the Greek system. I started a list of other Greek things I would boycott. On my shortlist were gyros, olives, and the removal of my Achilles tendon.

When I got Kathy's letter it seemed that my whole brief life had evaporated. So I did what all lovesick young men do. I got in my VW Bug and drove twenty hours from Humboldt State at the northern end of California to UCLA at the southern end. My assassin friend Doug came with me, and after two flat tires, lots of coffee, and several Jolt Colas, we made it to Los Angeles. I dropped Doug off somewhere and headed over to Kathy's sorority house, which was just off of Sunset Boulevard near UCLA. It was an immense house with stone creatures lining the front walk to intimidate any and all dumped boyfriends who approached.

I timidly took step after step, grabbed the door knocker, and tapped on the austere double door that rang with an air of impenetrability. I could hear the hollow reverberations inside, and from all appearances the house was utterly empty. But then, just as I was about to turn on my heels and retreat, I heard the faint sound of footsteps approaching the door. The door handle moved as I gulped and stood up tall. The door swung open, and there, like it was a perfect movie moment, was Kathy.

"Bob Goff?" she gasped in a mortified half shout, half moan.

Apparently, she was the only girl in the sorority house at the time and I had obviously caught her by surprise. Actually, her body language gave off kind of a combination plate of surprise, alarm, and I think I saw her throw up a little bit in her mouth.

"Come in," she stuttered, almost trying to retrieve the words as she spoke them. I *knew* it was over, but I went in anyway. You don't waste a twenty-hour road trip like that.

As I walked in, I was immediately taken by the grandeur of the huge sorority house. There was a marble entryway with bronze accents, marble walls with bronze fixtures, marble and bronze statues spread out like sentries in every direction. I guessed that the founder of the sorority must have invented marble and bronze or something. Just off the entryway, which we quickly transited, was another huge room anchored by a fireplace and a crackling fire and punctuated by a life-size bust of someone set on a table behind the couch. I figured it must have been a president or a prime minister but wasn't sure.

Kathy quickly and nervously ran me through the house for a quick tour—she always was polite. I fleetingly wondered how odd it must have been for her to have me there. As Kathy whisked me toward the front door again I passed the fireplace room, and what struck me as strange was that the bust in front of the fireplace was gone. It was just gone. *Really?* I thought. *What happened to the bronze bust?* Los Angeles was indeed an even more unusual place than I had originally thought. I was still scratching my head and puzzling over what was missing when Kathy hurried me out the door.

We walked to campus, where Kathy pointed to one building after another and told me about all the amazing experiences she was having and all the amazing people who went to UCLA. But we never really got around to the "why did you dump me?" conversation. This was not by accident, of course, because what I gathered later had occurred was this: Kathy and her "big brother" were the only ones at the sorority house that day and were snuggling on the couch in front of the fireplace when I knocked on the door. When Kathy said my name, the guy immediately froze and struck a chiseled pose as I walked by. Later, as Kathy was touring me around the house, he must've slipped out the front door. The chap kept looping around and passing by the two of us as we walked around campus. I guess the guy who ends up with the girl sometimes is just as insecure as the guy who gets dumped by her.

Later that afternoon, Kathy walked me out to my Volkswagen and I opened the door. I didn't really know what to say. I finally got out, "Did you really mean what you said in your letter about us?" It wasn't one of the deep, thoughtful, and probing questions I had practiced all the way down to Los Angeles, but it was all I could come up with at the time. "Yep," she confirmed as she patted me on the hand, stepped back, and muttered something about how she had to run to class.

I drove away dejected as I left UCLA and Kathy in the rearview mirror. Kathy married bronze boy, and I never really found out why I got upstaged. The fact that he was more handsome than me, had more potential than me, was smarter than me, and wasn't angling for a career that involved living in the woods, sleeping on a cot, eating TV dinners, or surfing may have been more than a feather in the balance. Nevertheless, it's still hard to come in second.

I've learned that God sometimes allows us to find ourselves in a place where we want something so bad that we can't see past it. Sometimes we can't even see God because of it. When we want something that bad, it's easy to mistake what we truly need for the thing we *really* want. When this sort of thing happens, and it seems to happen to everyone, I've found it's because what God has for us is obscured from view, just around another bend in the road.

In the Bible, the people following God had the same problem I did. They swapped the real thing for an image of the real thing. We target the wrong thing and our misdirected life's goal ends up looking like a girl or a wide-brimmed hat or a golden calf. All along, what God really wants for us is something much different, something more tailored to us.

It's in my nature, maybe all of our natures, to try to engineer things. So I skew the answers to get what I think I want. But when I do that, I also get what I don't want too, like a cot and a room full of guys. The first time I wanted someone to care for me as much as I cared for her, she picked someone else and I tried to talk her out of it. If I had been successful, I wouldn't have experienced love in the unique way that I have. I wouldn't have found who and what God tailor-made for me.

I'm kind of glad I didn't end up being a forest ranger or a surfer. I'm even glad things turned out the way they did after I drove away from UCLA. While painful at the time, I can see now, many years later when I look in the rearview mirror of my life, evidence of God's tremendous love and unfolding adventure for me. I've received many letters since then in my life that started out "Dear Bob." Some were letters so thick they had to be folded several times to fit in the envelope. They left me feeling as folded when I read their words with shattering disappointment. Still, whatever follows my "Dear Bobs" is often another reminder that God's grace comes in all shapes, sizes, and circumstances as God continues to unfold something magnificent in me.

And when each of us looks back at all the turns and folds God has allowed in our lives, I don't think it looks like a series of folded-over mistakes and do-overs that have shaped our lives. Instead, I think we'll conclude in the end that maybe we're all a little like human origami and the more creases we have, the better.

....

CHAPTER 6

"GO BUY YOUR BOOKS!"

I used to think God guided us by opening and closing doors,
but now I know sometimes God wants us to kick some doors down.

When I told my parents I was applying to law school, they looked at me like I was proposing to remove my own liver. You have to understand, my parents are both educators. I wasn't the smartest kid growing up. I'd bring home my grades and they'd look at me, wondering how the pear fell so far from the apple tree. When I graduated from high school, they gave me brochures for vocational schools that taught courses on engines, electronics, and plumbing. I think they pictured me installing low-voltage landscape lighting for the rest of my life. I did too.

I got into college and graduated with a degree in something I still know little about, and my grades reflected my wafer-thin understanding of the subject matter. It wasn't that I didn't try hard in college. I was just bored and searching for a good match for my particular wiring harness. I wanted to do things that would make a difference in the world. My professors, however, wanted me to do things that would make a difference in my grade point average. I spent most of college surfing and trying to figure out how I could help people in crisis here and abroad and make some kind of lasting contribution to the world. I didn't want to be a pastor or missionary—I knew God had better people set aside for that. So I decided that I was going to be a lawyer. I know, a lot of people think you can't love God or be a nice guy and still be a lawyer, but I was betting I could.

There is a big test called the LSAT you need to take before applying to law schools. All the schools look at your score on the test, then decide if they'll let you in. I knew the test was important, so I bought a paperback book on the LSAT at the local bookstore. It was about an inch thick, cost me $7.95, and I read it cover to cover at least three times before signing up for the exam. The book was an easy read, and it seemed simple enough. Most of the book was on how you sign up for the test.

When the big day for the exam arrived, I got to the test site an hour early. This was my shot at law school. The people sitting around me ranged from well-coiffed prep school types to late-night procrastinators still in their pajamas. Regardless of their outward appearance, though, everyone asked what review class I had taken to prepare for the LSAT. "Did you take the Princeton Review? Or was it BARBRI?" I heard four or five names of two-month-long review courses and estimated that the average height of prep materials everyone had was about five feet tall. It was apparent that I was woefully underprepared and my glazed-over look gave me away. "Hey, dude, are you okay?" one of the test-takers said, assuming a "surfer guy" persona because it probably seemed like the only way he could break through to me.

"Review class? There's a class you can take to prepare for this test?" was all I could choke out. I looked down at my measly dog-eared prep book, a mere 105 pages, and sighed as I threw it in a nearby trash can.

Since I had already paid the money, I went ahead and took the test. Weeks later, suffice it to say, I got the inevitable news. The LSAT crushed me. Despite the headwinds I was facing, I sent my applications to several law schools, you know, to give the admissions office a chuckle and break the monotony of sizing up the real law school candidates. I felt like I was basically making a small donation to each law school I applied to in the form of an application fee. I got lots of mail over the next few months brimming with lovely politeness that all ended in *no*. I get that a lot.

The really smart kids got letters back from the good law schools welcoming them and sometimes even giving them scholarships to sweeten their offers. The medium smart kids got regular admissions from the regular law schools. And the just plain smart kids got put on waiting lists. I got none of the above. From anyone. I think some of the schools didn't write back because they figured we both just kind of knew. Some rejection letters I received even returned my application check. Either they didn't have the heart to take my money knowing I had *zero* chance of getting in, or they figured that with my score that low, I should save every penny I had.

There was one problem with all of this. You see, I wanted to be a lawyer so I could make an impact in the world, which meant I had to graduate from law school. With no defensible case for admission anywhere, I still decided I wouldn't take no for an answer.

I knew the law school I wanted to attend. So about a week before classes started, I went over to the great big hall with the dean's office and admissions staff. I introduced myself at the front desk, and they seemed pleased to meet the person who had been phoning them incessantly to confirm that indeed he really didn't get in. I walked to the dean's large office door, knocked, and sheepishly entered his austere room covered with bookshelves and intelligence. The dean of the law school stood up and greeted me with a reserved but polite formality that fit his position and title.

I shoved my hand forward confidently like they say in the books to do and introduced myself.

"Hello, I'm Bob Goff, and I applied to get into your law school," I said. "I applied because I want to be a lawyer and make a real difference in the world."

The dean smiled politely, didn't say a word, and remained standing. Apparently this wasn't enough to convince him.

"There's a problem, however. You see, I didn't get an acceptance letter. For that matter, I didn't even get a rejection letter. I didn't get put on a waiting list either. But I want to get into your law school and graduate, or I can't be a lawyer someday." I thought I had framed my situation pretty well.

The dean shook my hand again as he said, "This is a competitive program, and unfortunately we have to turn down many qualified candidates." Mercifully, he skipped the part about me not being one of them.

"It was nice to meet you," he said, still shaking my hand. Once he broke his grasp, he put his hand on my shoulder and started moving toward the door. His body language left nothing to be misinterpreted.

"I hope you have a nice day," he offered as he began to slowly close the door. I had the chance to say one last thing before the dean disappeared into his paneled office. So I stopped the closing door with my foot and said, "You have the power to let me in. I know all you have to tell me is, 'Go buy your books,' and I could be a student in the law school. It's that simple. You just need to say those words." He gave me a half grin indicating he thought it was a cute idea but wasn't going to happen. Then the door closed. I'm sure he thought he was finished with me and could go on with the important business of training the law students who actually had potential.

There was a bench in front of the dean's office. It reminded me of the bench I frequently warmed in the principal's office during elementary school. There were five days left before law school started, and I decided I would park myself on that bench every day. Every time he passed by, I would say to the dean, "All you have to do is tell me, 'Go buy your books.'" It was a last-ditch plan from a determined surfer.

The first time the dean walked by, he asked me why I was still there. I told him that while I understood they had turned down my application. I knew he had the power to let me in. All he had to do was say the words, "Go get your books." He smiled at me and walked away.

I had a lot of time to think sitting on my bench, day in, day out. I thought about instances in the Bible where all it took was saying the word to make it happen. Jesus would say a word and people would be healed and He just said, "Come" to a guy named Peter and that guy ended up walking on water for heaven's sake. There was even a time when Jesus was on His way to a soldier's house to heal a servant, but the soldier said all Jesus had to do was say the word and his ailing servant would be better. As I sat on my bench, I believed words still had power when they are said by the right people.

With four days to go before school started I was back at my post bright and early in the morning. Every time the dean passed in or out of his office, I would say, "Just tell me to buy my books." He'd just nod, sometimes shake his head, and sometimes completely ignore me and then walk away.

The same thing occurred three days, two days, and then one day to go before law school started. I had missed the 1960s, but I still felt like this was a sit-in and I was part of it. By the third or fourth day on the bench, I knew everything about the dean's schedule. I knew when he took his bathroom breaks, his daily meetings, when he left for the gym and returned. Every time he darkened the door of his office, I'd be sitting there smiling and waiting for him to say the words, words that could change everything for me.

At dawn on the day law school started, I sprang out of bed. I just knew this was going to be the big day for me. At seven o'clock in the morning, I was on my appointed bench. I watched all of the smart kids arrive, bustling around and sizing each other up. Their high-functioning din ricocheted off the marble walls and columns. I sat there eager to hear the words, but I didn't even see the dean the entire day. I was dejected. My plan to make it into law school before the opening day hadn't worked. So I took a lap around the halls and decided that if I couldn't make it into law school before it started, I'd just get in afterward and catch up.

The dean passed by at least a dozen times in the course of the second day. "Just tell me to buy my books," I'd say each time. And each time, nothing. Day two of law school ended, as did day three. I was falling behind at law school and I wasn't even admitted. Day four, still nothing. On day five, for the first time, my hope was starting to crater as I dragged myself to my perch. All the smart kids had settled into their routines and the rigors of law school, and the only noises that echoed off of the walls in the large marbled hall were mine. I mused in my boredom about what it would sound like if I brought my Fender Stratocaster in and played a couple of my favorite Doobie Brothers riffs. I decided I'd save that for graduation day.

Late in the afternoon, I heard the familiar footfall of the dean walking toward the door. I glanced at my watch. This was a little early for him to be leaving but a little late for his midafternoon bathroom stop. There was nothing about this guy's schedule I didn't know. And then the footsteps stopped.

Without a lot of fanfare, the dean turned the corner from his office, and as usual, I prepared to say, "Just tell me to go buy my books." Something was different this time, though, because instead of avoiding me and walking away without saying anything, the dean just stood there towering over me. There was a long pause. The dean looked me squarely in the eyes, gave me a wink, and said the four words that changed my life forever: "*Go buy your books.*"

And I did.

I once heard somebody say that God had closed a door on an opportunity they had hoped for. But I've always wondered if, when we want to do something that we know is right and good, God places that desire deep in our hearts because He wants it for us and it honors Him. Maybe there are times when we think a door has been closed and, instead of misinterpreting the circumstances, God wants us to kick it down. Or perhaps just sit outside of it long enough until somebody tells us we can come in.

Words can launch us. We don't need to be a dean to say words that change everything for someone. Instead, God made it so that ordinary people like you and me can launch each other. In fact, I wonder if we can launch people better than a dean because we're ordinary. I believe it's true that the right people can say words that can change everything. And guess what? We're the ones who can say them.

It's been a number of years since I sat on the dean's bench trying to get into law school. These days, I do a number of things, but one of them is to serve as an adjunct professor at Pepperdine Law School, where I get to teach nonprofit law to some fantastic law students. They're the really smart kids who got the letters that said yes. Now I'm the one who gets to speak words of life and encouragement to them.

I get a chuckle when I pass by the dean's office on the way to teach class, and I think about a different dean's office I sat in front of at a different law school, hoping for the chance to be a lawyer someday. Every time I get a chance, I find a student who is hoping to get into my class but the school didn't let them in for some reason. And without a lot of fanfare I find where they are sitting and stop. I look them squarely in the eyes, give them a wink, and tell them . . .

"Go buy your books."

CHAPTER 7

SWEET MARIA

I used to think Jesus motivated us with ultimatums,
but now I know He pursues us in love.

Do you remember falling in love the first time? I do. I was a Young Life leader in college along with my buddy Doug. Young Life is an outfit that does a great job with high school kids introducing them to Jesus of Nazareth without making it a big religious deal. A girl just out of college named Maria came to help Doug and me because we didn't have any college-age women leaders. I was standing up front playing songs on the guitar when Maria walked in the room. When I saw her, I immediately broke a string, leaned over, and whispered to Doug, "That's Mrs. Goff." I asked Maria later what she remembers about that night, and she says she doesn't remember whispering anything to anybody about me. If Jesus has taught me anything, though, it's that sometimes you can really want to know somebody and it takes them forever to want to know you back.

The day I saw Maria was ten days before Valentine's Day. And since I had already secretly claimed her as my bride, I figured I'd better let her get to know me. You know that feeling where you don't know what to do with yourself? Everything reminds you of that person. A painting, a sunset, children playing, a couple holding hands, a paperclip, my wristwatch, everything. Yet thinking about them just isn't enough; you just need to do something, anything.

Maria worked at an advertising agency on the twelfth floor of a high-rise office building downtown. I had known Maria for a whole week and a half, so I did the most sensible thing I could think of: make her a huge Valentine's Day card. I got two huge sheets of four-foot-by-eight-foot cardboard and glued the edges together. A perfect envelope. I made a stamp the size of a doormat and put it on the envelope upside down. (Guys, you know that means "I love you," right? If not, back to finishing school for you.) Inside, I took another four-foot-by-eight-foot piece of cardboard and wrote, "Maria, will you be my Valentine?" Simple. Straightforward. Not too hard to spell. I really wanted to write, "Maria, will you marry me?" but it would have been a little early. Proposals are definitely week three material.

I borrowed a guy's truck and drove my gigantic card downtown and into the garage of the high-rise. I struggled to get the card into the elevator and drew more than a few odd looks and smiles. The elevator sped me upward. I felt so excited I thought I was going to faint. But I didn't want to crumple the card, so I pulled myself together. Wouldn't Maria think this was just about the greatest Valentine's Day card she'd ever received? Wouldn't she know how nuts I was for her? Wouldn't she like me back? This was going to be just great. She was going to love it!

The elevator slowed to a stop and sounded the bell as the doors opened. It took me awhile to get the card out of the elevator. The bell started ringing more urgently. It probably sounded like someone had installed a Vegas-style slot machine next to the emergency phone, but it was just me struggling to get the card out of the elevator. Word must have spread in the office about the guy with the big card stuck in the elevator because, within a few seconds, a small crowd gathered in the lobby. I heard them wonder out loud if they should have the fire department bring the Jaws of Life to get me out.

Once I got clear of the doors, this small gaggle stared at me like I was wearing diving gear—fins, snorkel, scuba tank, the whole bit. For the first time, I started thinking that maybe this wasn't such a good idea. But it was too late. After being paged, Maria came around the corner and saw me standing there with a big dumb grin, floppy ears, and a gigantic, overambitious card. I don't think a group of guys stomping out Riverdance behind me would have been more of a shock to her. Maria was absolutely mortified. It set our courtship back about six months—bare minimum.

During the next six months, I was trigger-locked on Maria while she treated me with a polite distance. She would barely talk to me and I was told, hopefully with a good dose of sarcasm, that the sight of cardboard made her run. But I was undaunted, despite the fact that a column of smoke was still rising from smoldering embers where I crashed and burned on Valentine's

Day. I didn't quite know what to do with myself, but I had to do something to express what I was feeling inside. Then I remembered: I knew where she parked her car!

I decided to start each day by making Maria a peanut butter and jelly sandwich, and I put it under the windshield wiper of her car. Why? I'm not quite sure. It was like I was sandwich-stalking her. Sometimes I would even put notes in the sandwiches.

I know all this sounds crazy, but if you got to know me I bet you wouldn't think so. Maria probably thought that I was weird. But weird can be safe too, and my love was a weird, safe love. Fortunately, Maria understood that for some of us—most of us—the language of love is laced with whimsy. It sometimes borders on the irrational. Like I've been saying, though, love is a *do* thing. It's an energy that has to be dissipated.

I lived in a beach house in San Diego during law school. It was more like a shack actually. It was next to a laundry mat, and a couple of us homely looking guys lived together and split cheap rent. There was a house across the alley from us that was often rented by female Young Life leaders, so I angled for Maria to get a room. It turned out that the three homely guys in our house were interested in the three beautiful girls in their house. Eventually, each of the guys married each of the girls—one apiece. No kidding. It just so happened that whichever girl slept on the bottom bunk at their house was always the next to get married to one of us. Looking back, I wish I'd have snuck in and made the other mattresses a little less comfortable because Maria never seemed to move into that bottom bunk. I suspected that she had seen the trend and had perhaps opted to sleep on the couch or floor rather than risk ending up with me.

During the time that I was trying to get Maria to notice me, I was studying for the bar exam. She would come over to say hello, and I would be curled up in the fetal position. Toward the end of law school, the professor told us to look around because every third person in the row wouldn't pass the exam. No matter which end of the row I started counting from, I was always the third guy! I'm not one for superstition or anything, but there was a real sense of portent in that seating arrangement. Never mind that I'd been studying for three years.

Adding to the pressure, I didn't want to ask Maria to marry me unless I had passed the bar exam. I'm not sure why this was a self-imposed prerequisite. I guess I didn't want her stuck with the guy who constantly mumbled about how "the seventh time's the charm" while duplicating keys in a parking lot kiosk. What made it worse is that my roommate Kevin was the top student at the law school and was about the smartest guy in the whole world. His girl couldn't wait for him to pop the question. No one seemed to be wondering how the bar exam would work out for Kevin. I, on the other hand, was scanning the want ads as a fallback.

Somehow I squeaked by the California bar exam the first time. It was finally time to ask sweet Maria to marry me. I arranged to borrow someone's brand-new, half-million-dollar yacht. I hatched a plan to sail to a secluded place where Maria and I would take my tiny, thrashed sailboat and read books together. Books she'd bought us about friendship, actually. By now, I sensed that Maria was either overcome with pity or was actually starting to like me. She probably also intuited that if she married anyone else I'd likely live under her house just to be near her. She must've decided liking me back would be less complicated. And less creepy.

I decorated the yacht with a rainbow's worth of colored crepe paper. And then—it started raining. The rainstorm hit with a vengeance, drenching my proposal plans and leaving the brand-new yacht with colors smeared across the deck and hull like a very expensive tie-dyed T-shirt. I didn't spend the day proposing to Maria and dreaming about a life together. I spent it scrubbing soggy-colored disappointment off some guy's boat.

Although the first plan had imploded, I was still going to get the girl. I had an idea.

There was a turn-of-the-century building next to the Hotel del Coronado, and the roof was enclosed by this thing called a "widow's walk." It was more of an architectural feature, really, but to me it created a tiny rooftop restaurant—one that was eight feet by eight feet. Layers of dust, broken chairs, old napkins, and outdated menus were strewn about. But I had high hopes for it. I described my failed boat caper and floundering marriage proposal dreams to the building owner. The guy could see how desperate I was, and I was doing my best to look forlorn, which wasn't hard. So he let me move the chairs and set up a small table, two chairs, and some candlesticks in the tiny room.

Later that night as the storm raged outside, I led Maria up to the little room I had readied. When Maria and I finished dinner, I got down on a knee and asked, "Maria, will you . . . ?" Then the emotion of the moment was just too much for me and I couldn't talk anymore. As has been one of Sweet Maria's many outstanding characteristics ever since—she helped me finish what I had started, and said, "Yes."

These days I continue to tell Sweet Maria that I am much

more experienced at loving her than she is at loving me—because among other things, I've been at it a couple of years longer than she's been. She usually teases me about the lame Valentine's card and asks me what in the world I was thinking with the sandwiches under the wipers each morning.

I love my wife very much and I always will. For the past twenty-five years she's been my muse. My love for her and her love for me is the fire that warms our family. But the reason I wanted to tell you this story is that it has to do with another thing I learned following Jesus. Because God made me to love Maria, and because God made it so I had to convince her to love me back, He gave me a very real way to understand what is happening in the universe.

Because of our love for each other, I understand just a little more how God has pursued me in creative and whimsical ways, ways that initially did not get my attention. Nevertheless, He wouldn't stop. That's what love does—it pursues blindly, unflinchingly, and without end. When you go after something you love, you'll do anything it takes to get it, even if it costs everything.

Maria and I spend our summers in a beautiful part of British Columbia. We've built a house on the water so people who are tired or need to work something out can come and find rest. The house is at the end of an inlet that might be the most beautiful place on earth. And one of my favorite things to do in the inlet is to take a boat back to a place called Chatterbox Falls. To get there, you have to go through a fjord with rock cliffs jutting up from the water thousands of feet on both sides until they disappear beneath huge white glaciers. There's a mountain too, a beautiful mountain called One Eye. You can see it on your left as you race across the water to Chatterbox.

Sometimes we go right by it and I don't pay any attention, but other times it strikes me with a power that causes me to stop the boat and stare in amazement. To me, it's proof that God loves us and pursues us and does things to get our attention like giving me my mind to perceive beauty and then wooing me with the beauty of that fjord and that mountain.

I've seen mountains with peaks that look like the head of a horse, and others that look like eagle wings stretched out in flight. But to me, when I stop, amazed once again at the ways God loves and pursues us, and kind of squint a little, One Eye looks a lot like a guy getting out of an elevator with a giant Valentine's Day card.

CHAPTER 8

....

WEDDING CAKE

I used to think being a believer was enough,
but now I know Jesus wants us to participate,
no matter what condition we're in.

When I got married, we didn't have any money at all. I was just out of law school and was volunteering as a Young Life leader at one of the local high schools. I think after I sold my rusty Volkswagen we had about three dollars to spend for each person who was coming to the wedding, maybe less. We didn't get many flowers; instead we got lots of balloons and we found a caterer who felt sorry enough for us to give us some food for cheap. The cake was going to be a big problem, though. Sweet Maria had checked around and a cake was going to cost more than we had for the whole wedding. Then I remembered there was a kid in Young Life whose dad owned a bakery. I asked how big of a cake we could get for about $150 and he said he could make one that would be about four stories tall. That would do.

The wedding went as weddings do. I said "I do," she said "I do," and we ran down the aisle. The reception was held at a very swanky clubhouse on a lake in Fairbanks Ranch. In order to live in Fairbanks Ranch I think you need to have invented medicine or energy or something. I was a young lawyer and my boss had purchased a home in the area. With the purchase came the right to use the clubhouse on the lake twice a year—for free. That was just inside our price range. My boss was a generous guy and secured the venue, and we showed up with our bags of balloons, the caterer, and the pasta salad. Because we couldn't afford much in terms of food to serve, we had the caterers put up a lot of props that couldn't be eaten but made it look like quite a feast. Big loaves of bread and huge cheese wheels lingered just out of reach and towered like mountains over our pasta salad.

When we got to the reception, I saw that my high-school-age friend had already arrived from the bakery with the cake. What caught my eye was that he was assembling our four-story cake on top of an AV cart in the parking lot. *Is that how it's done?* I wondered. He had put all the pillars in place and was already assembling the third floor of our white cake skyscraper as we parked. It looked very impressive as he continued to assemble it in the parking lot like he was building downtown all over again. He had everything up except a crane, scaffolding, and road cones.

I was walking my new bride toward the entrance to the reception as he carefully put the bride and groom ornaments on the pinnacle of his masterpiece. The happy plastic couple towered above the parking lot as they surveyed all that was theirs below them. They would certainly not be eaten at the reception and they stood with a confidence that comes with knowing that. As my young friend started wheeling the high-rise cake toward the clubhouse on the AV cart, its wobbling back left wheel somehow drew attention to what a bad idea it was. Then predictably, as if it was unfolding in slow motion, the cart hit a small rock and abruptly stopped, but the upper levels of the cake didn't. In rapid succession, each layer of the cake fell off of its pillars and headed toward the parking lot. Three splats later, most of our wedding cake was lying on the asphalt in a pile. We all just kind of stood there without speaking, looking at the pile of cake in stunned silence, the bride and groom ornaments laying silently on top looking like they had just lost a massive food fight.

Calling for some quick thinking as the guests were about to arrive at any minute, I pulled my shell-shocked young baker aside between two parked cars and we hatched a plan. He scooped the cake together and jumped back in his well-used Subaru. Thirty minutes later, he was back with a bucket of shredded cake and an even bigger bucket of freshly made icing from the bakery. In the back room, he iced the shards of cake back into shape, restacked it and—yes, I am a little embarrassed to say—we served it up. Gravel, small bits of asphalt, and all.

Like that cake, my life is full of small rocks, pieces of asphalt, broken and unrepaired relationships, and unwanted debris. But somehow God allows us each to be served up anyway. Jesus talked to social outcasts, loose women, lawyers like me, and religious people and said they would not just be so many decorations or window treatments, but He would serve them up as well. He said this was true even though we're full of the kind of grit that accumulates over the span of a life and quite a few parking lots.

The only thing that Jesus said He couldn't serve up were people who were full of themselves or believed the lie that they were who they used to be before they met Him.

Jesus seemed to say that all we would need to do is to scrape together the pieces of our lives that had fallen on the ground, bring those pieces to Him, and He would start using them. Jesus didn't say He would ice over the grit of faults and failures either; He said He would use us in spite of the grit and faults and failures. What we would have to do is decide to move from the parking lot to the party. And He said we can't do that by just believing all the right stuff anymore; Jesus said He'd help us start doing the right stuff.

At some point I stopped staring at the pile of broken cake on the asphalt that was my life and decided to get some skin in the game. My life had not been shattered into many pieces by a massive tragedy, but it consisted of as many disorganized pieces as it would if it had been. I simply decided that I wasn't going to let the residual rocks and small pieces of gravel get in the way of me getting served up and used. It has always seemed to me that broken things, just like broken people, get used more; it's probably because God has more pieces to work with.

Jesus talked about lawyers a lot too. None of it was very flattering, actually. He usually lumped lawyers in with liars and people who didn't speak the truth. Jesus said they were getting in the way of people knowing God, which is a really bad thing. He said the same thing about religious people too, sometimes in the same sentence. But He also talked about everybody else and what He said to them is that we all could be used, not just when we're broken, but especially *because* we're broken.

I've tried to build a few things in my life. I took what I

thought were great ideas, I stacked them neatly on pillars, put them on my AV cart, and rolled them out. I've hit my share of rocks too, and those rocks have sent parts of my dreams hurling. Yet Jesus continues to select broken and splattered people not just as followers but as participants. He called people like me who can't even figure out which end of a plastic bag to open His hands, He called people who trip every day His feet, and He called people who can't figure out which way to turn a screw to tighten it or even stack a cake correctly the ones who would build a kingdom. And then, if we're willing, He serves us up—rocks, small bits of asphalt, and all.

CHAPTER 9

....

JUST SAY YES

I used to think you had to be special for God to use you,
but now I know you simply need to say yes.

love playing practical jokes on my buddies. My friend Doug made the big mistake of telling me one time where he was going to celebrate his tenth wedding anniversary. He had rented the penthouse suite at a fancy hotel and was going to surprise his bride with an overnight stay. It was way too tempting for me *not* to come up with a prank.

A few days later, Sweet Maria and I went to the fancy hotel and checked in as if we were Doug and his wife. I walked up to the clerk at the front desk and confidently said that I was Doug and wanted to know if our room was ready. The room was prepaid so they tossed me the room key and asked me if there was anything they could do for me. I told them there indeed was and I'd be calling down from the room soon—I had a list. Sweet Maria and I skipped to the elevator that rocketed us to the top floor of the hotel to a huge pair of doors. We each grabbed a handle and turned at the same time. We were greeted by a magnificent room, the kind that a professional interior decorator had dressed from top to bottom. On the far side of the room was a wall of windows with a stunning view of the city on one side and the bay on the other. It was a spectacular view, and the room was enormous. I think it must have had its own zip code.

I picked up the phone, which went straight to the front desk, and we ordered room service. We had lobster for the first course. For dinner: lightly sautéed vegetables over rice and salmon. For dessert: actually, I'm not sure what the dessert was, but the table-side server set it on fire. It was so cool we ordered seconds. We turned on some beautiful music and danced. We laughed. We had them send up ice cream—just because we could. After we had finished soaking in the panoramic views and the last of the plates had been cleared, we signed the waiter up for a big tip, tidied the room, and split.

When Doug and his wife checked in to the hotel several hours later, they were led to their magnificent room by a slightly confused but compliant bellman. *Hadn't they already checked in?* What a fantastic night they had, I'm told. The next day, when Doug went to check out, the concierge slid the bill across the counter. Doug's eyes popped when he saw a four-hundred-dollar room service bill.

From our house the next morning I was imagining what

must have been his futile protest over and over in my head as I smiled. "Hey, wait! I didn't order room service! I didn't order seconds! *Extra* ice cream? I would never leave a tip this big!"

Then the nickel must have dropped when he realized I had pranked him as he groaned under his breath, *"Bob!"*

Doug's been trying to get back at me for years. But he can't, because I'm a lawyer. You don't get into and through law school like I did without gaining a few street smarts.

A few years later, however, I received a phone call from a fellow who introduced himself through a heavy accent as the ambassador from Uganda. I immediately thought, *Yeah, right, and you have my home phone number.* I knew it had to be Doug or someone he put up to the task. I listened intently as the caller spoke and I played along.

"So, Bob. I'm aware of what you have been doing in Uganda over the past several years with the children in the jails and with the judiciary. I'm very pleased and want to thank you on behalf of the president. In fact, I am so pleased that I want to know if you would consider something." I couldn't wait to hear what Doug had cooked up.

"I want to know if you will be counsel for the Republic of Uganda."

Counsel? I thought. *Uganda needs a lawyer? Why? Does someone owe them money? And why would they want me to be their legal counsel anyway?*

No matter. This was just Doug's weak attempt to get even for the hotel incident. I covered the phone and whispered to Sweet Maria, "It's Doug. He's playing a prank on me. I'll tell you more in a second, but you're about to hear me say yes a lot, okay?"

Yes after yes left my lips, and the conversation ended with

Doug or his hired gun saying he was leaving for Uganda and would call me back in about two months when he returned.

"Yes, of course," I replied. "Have a nice trip. Great to talk to you. Say hello to everyone from me."

The next two months were busy and passed in a blink. I hadn't given much thought to Doug's call and kind of figured that his joke had gone its course. And then the phone rang.

The caller introduced himself again as the ambassador from Uganda. Through his thick accent, which was a spot-on match to the voice from the first call, he said, "Bob, I only have a few minutes. I want you to know that you need to meet me in New York on Saturday." I remembered that I had decided to say yes no matter how outlandish the request was.

"New York? Yes, you bet." I was feeling some moxie and said, "I was hoping you'd ask. See you there!" The person with the accent gave me the address of one of the nicer hotels in Manhattan.

I was in for an adventure, for sure. But to drop everything and hop on a plane all to make my friend feel like we were even—it was a lot to concede, even for me. But a yes is a yes, so off I went.

When I got off the plane at Kennedy Airport a few days later and headed downtown to the hotel, I was thinking, *I may have gotten Doug for a four-hundred-dollar lobster dinner, but he's getting me back and then some. Look at me. I just flew across the country to New York so I could supposedly be Uganda's lawyer.* I shook my head and quietly chuckled as the taxi driver drove me into the city. Getting out of the car at the hotel, I fully expected to pick up a note card in the lobby from Doug that said, "You came all this way. Go ahead and get the lobster—it's on me!" I was milling about in the hotel lobby and saw an entourage pull up with little Ugandan flags waving above the headlights. Then several members of Uganda's government strode into the lobby. I hadn't even considered that this could be real, so I was shocked. I hesitated even identifying myself and thought I could slip back to the airport unnoticed.

Ambassador Kamuninwire came bouncing up. "I'm Ambassador Kamuninwire."

"Of course you are!" I replied as I gave him a hug. The ambassador was a jolly, brilliant, and affable man who looked to be in his late fifties. He had a heavy yet wonderfully British accent, as do most Ugandans. He isn't the kind of guy who walks—he gallops. He has the swagger of a high school quarterback and the smile of a pastor. He is the kind of guy you instantly feel like you've known for years.

The ambassador gathered the dignitaries from Uganda around him and with one arm around my shoulder introduced me. "This is our new consul for the Republic of Uganda."

"Consul?" I laughed out loud. "You said that you wanted me to be 'counsel,' you know, a lawyer, right?" The ambassador didn't skip a beat.

He let out another one of his jolly laughs. "No, Bob, I said consul, not counsel! We want you to be a diplomat representing the Republic of Uganda to the United States." He continued, "I've got the paperwork all completed. All you need to do is give me a couple of passport pictures and I'll submit it to Uganda's parliament for approval."

I did what I told Sweet Maria I'd do every time he asked me to do something. I said yes.

Four months passed without any further updates, but then word came that the parliament for the Republic of Uganda had approved the appointment. I got a call shortly thereafter from someone with a stern voice, the kind of voice that doesn't approve of monkey business and wears dark blue suits. It was the State Department informing me of the customary FBI background check being done on my file. "I have a file? How cool is that?" Apparently all of my misdeeds must have been overlooked, and I was approved by the State Department for appointment as consul for the Republic of Uganda to the United States. My diplomatic credentials were issued within weeks, and my family and I planned for the big ceremony.

At this point, someone told me about the perks of being a diplomat. First, I would get some really cool license plates. With those, I can literally park anywhere. On the sidewalk, on the grass, on second base in Fenway Park, in your garage, wherever. Second, I get a set of Ugandan flags to put on my car. I pictured those diplomatic license plates and a couple of Ugandan flags on my ride. Sweet! Finally, and definitely the coolest part, is that you get a card from the State Department that gives you diplomatic immunity. I wasn't exactly sure what diplomatic immunity meant, so I asked around to see if I could kill someone. Not someone important, of course, but someone normal—like Doug. I never got a call back on that question, so I'm operating under the assumption that I can.

I think God sometimes uses the completely inexplicable events in our lives to point us toward Him. We get to decide each time whether we will lean in toward what is unfolding and say yes or back away. The folks who were following Jesus in Galilee got to decide the same thing each day because there was no road map, no program, and no certainty. All they had was this person, an idea, and an invitation to come and see.

I like the passage in Scripture where God chooses Moses to lead. Moses puts up a fight, saying nobody will follow him. God gives him three miracles to perform to establish confidence with his audience, but Moses protests again, saying he stutters and can't speak and asks God to please choose somebody else. When Moses protests yet again, God gets a little angry and instructs Moses to take Aaron with him. I don't think it was because Moses needed Aaron but because Moses mistakenly thought he had to be somebody important in order to be part of what God was going to do.

I can relate. I'm the guy checking into my buddy's room to spend a bunch of his money on room service. Then I'm the guy who thinks he's being pranked. Then I'm the guy who thinks he's being asked to be a lawyer when really he's being asked to be a diplomat. Then I'm the guy who is sticking Ugandan flags on his car. *Am I the right guy?* I don't know, but I'm the guy being asked, and the last thing I want to do is miss an opportunity or make God mad, so I just keep saying yes. Maybe God is doing some inexplicable things in your life. Each of us gets to decide every time whether to lean in or step back—to say yes, ignore it, or tell God why He has the wrong person.

There's this beautiful story in the Bible about a guy named Joseph that a friend of mine named Don tells all the time. The story of Joseph has more turns in it than a mountain road in Colorado. It's an emotional roller coaster, but it ends up with Joseph being second-in-command in Egypt. And twice at the end of the book Joseph says that the reason God put him where He did was to save many lives. And if you think about it, the reason God chose Moses was to save many lives. And the same goes for Jonah and Peter, all the apostles, and Jesus. And us, too, for that matter. We were all meant to save many lives. God is always trying to save lives, and it seems like He usually uses the least likely people to do it.

So the next time God asks you to do something that is completely inexplicable, something you're sure is a prank because it requires a decision or courage that's way over your pay grade, something that might even save lives, say yes. You never know—there might be some cool flags in it for you.

....

CHAPTER 10

THE INTERVIEWS

I used to think I had to be somebody important to accomplish things, but now I know Jesus uses ordinary people more.

When the kids were growing up, we didn't have a television in the house connected to a cable or an antenna. If something bad happened in the world, I wanted the kids to hear about it from me. Whether it was news that the president had a girlfriend or that a plane hit a building, I thought the kids should hear about it from their parents. On the morning of September 11, 2001, I rushed home before the kids left for school and gathered them around our dining room table and told them what had happened. Like everyone else, we struggled for words to describe to our kids why such a thing would occur. We talked about the presence of evil and the presence of good and how good ultimately wins. It was hard to really feel it, though, as I was mouthing the words.

After talking for a while, I asked the kids this: "If you had five minutes in front of a group of world leaders, what would you ask them to help make sense of life, faith, hope, and the events that are unfolding around them?" I admit it was a dorky dad thing to do, but I had each of them write down what they would ask on a piece of paper.

Adam, who was seven at the time, loved having people over to the house. I wasn't surprised when Adam said that he would ask the world leaders if they wanted to come over to our house. When you're seven, there's nothing like having someone over to play with to get to know them better. Maybe, Adam thought, having the leaders over to the house could facilitate better understanding between each of these leaders and they would become better friends. I told Adam I thought his idea was a great one, and he wrote it down on a piece of paper.

Richard was next. He said he would ask each of the world leaders what they were hoping for. The idea was that if world leaders knew what each other were hoping for, then perhaps they could start hoping for the same things. Rich reasoned that the problem was no one knew what other people were quietly hoping for. Richard's idea sounded super as well, so he wrote it down.

Lindsey was the last to go and had listened to her brothers' ideas. As the oldest, she was the precocious one and had written down her idea already, and I read it out loud. If the leaders couldn't come over to our house for a visit, then what if she and her brothers went to their houses to ask them what they were hoping for? Even better, she had written, all three kids should do a video interview with the leaders so they could share it with all the others. That way, each of these leaders would know what the others were hoping for and maybe find they were hoping for the same things. I was amazed at what fantastic imaginations these kids had. They didn't even consider that what they were asking for was absurd or naive. Or that they needed to be famous or powerful to ask their questions. Perhaps what the leaders would prefer was a few innocent kids asking innocent questions of them.

I had the kids put their ideas together in one letter. Then we downloaded the names of every president, prime minister, or dictator of every country in the world from the CIA website. We felt like we were hacking into NORAD; it was so cool. The information was all there; we just needed to figure out the addresses. The kids decided they didn't just want to write to a couple of the leaders. They wanted to write to *all* of them. *Heck, why not give them all an equal shot at meeting these great kids?* I thought

Next, we got a post office box. Mostly because we didn't want Ahmadinejad knowing where we lived. Maria and I also made a deal with the kids. We told them that we'd mail all of the letters, and if we got even a single yes from one of the world leaders to their request for a meeting, we would take them!

We mailed the letters. Lots of them. Hundreds and hundreds of them. We waited a week or two and then every day after school, we would check the kids' post office box for any mail. It wasn't long before responses started coming. It was slow at first, maybe one or two a day. But then dozens started streaming in every day from all over the globe. We got a small globe of planet Earth and stuck a pin in every country whose leader responded. It wasn't long before our little earth was peppered with hundreds of pins and looked like it was undergoing serious acupuncture treatments.

Pretty much every letter the kids received back said thanks but no thanks. But the wording was so eloquent that it still made the kids feel great. (Law school admissions offices could learn a thing or two from these guys.) For instance, Tony Blair, prime minister of England at the time, handwrote something to the effect of "jolly good idea about meeting." He still said no, but it was cool knowing he at least thought it was a nice idea. None of us were really sure what *jolly good* meant exactly, but the kids guessed it must be a nice way to say no. From then on, when I asked them to do their homework or the dishes they would say, "Jolly good!"

It was a Tuesday like any other day, and after school the kids and I swung by the post office to pick up their mail. They came springing out the door of the post office like they always did with a wad of letters wrapped in a huge rubber band. They jumped in the car and divided the letters between them in the backseat. There were several more nos but also a letter from the State House in Bulgaria. They opened it up together and started reading. Then came a shriek and from somewhere in the backseat the words that changed everything.

"We're invited to the palace to meet!" the kids roared in unison.

"Of course you are!" I answered.

A day or two later, an envelope from the prime minister of Switzerland arrived, inviting them to Bern. Then a letter came from the president of Israel, inviting the kids to come to Jerusalem. Over the following weeks, they didn't just get one yes—they got *twenty-nine*. Maria and I didn't know what to do, so we did the best thing we could think of. We began a family training program to spruce up on our manners. One of the yeses came from a real live prince, so we taught the kids how to bow and curtsy too.

Maria and I had a promise to keep to the kids. So we told the school that we were pulling them out for a grand caper. Some of their teachers had a cow when we said how long we'd be gone and one wrote me a letter about it. I opened it, wrote "Tough!" on it, sent it back, and we left.

Now, if leaders were talking to grown-ups like me, they would talk about boring things like having more jobs, gross domestic product, better schools, and more roads. You know, the kind of stuff crafted for public consumption. But they weren't talking to me; they were talking to our kids. Sweet Maria and I were just roadies carrying the cameras.

What would happen more often than not is that the kids would begin in an official reception room and have an official meeting with the leader. But then the leaders would realize these were just kids who had no agenda other than to be friends and they would invite us back to their private offices where they could just talk as friends. The kids would ask questions about the leaders' families, how they got into public service, and what their hopes were for the future. The leaders would talk about their children and grandchildren, what they were doing when they were our kids' ages, and their dreams of friendships between people from our two countries.

In one country, the kids were meeting across from the former Communist Party Headquarters and were escorted past guards wearing holsters with some serious guns peeking just out of their coats. Doors were opened to a large reception room with dozens of chairs lining a huge table that must have been fifty feet long. In the room was an interpreter who greeted the kids warmly, and after a short time, we heard heavy steps coming down the hallway announcing the arrival of the leader.

A stout man with a grave expression entered the room, came toward us down the length of the table, and sat down. There was an electrified hush in the room. The leader peered at the kids and said in Russian, "Children, I'm more nervous meeting you than if I were meeting with President Bush right now." There was a long pause as the translator finished the sentence in English.

"And when I get nervous," he grumbled through his accent and paused, "I get hungry!"

With these words, his demeanor completely transformed. He clapped his hands and palace servants flooded into the room with trays and trays of kid food, the kind you would eat at a sleepover. Our end of the table was soon covered with strawberry tarts, pastries you could hardly see because of all the icing and cherries, unknown delights doused with whipped cream, and mountains of ice cream. The leader sat back and grinned and watched the kids' faces beam with excitement. "Eat!" he shouted as he raised his arms to present this feast fit for child kings.

The kids tried to practice their manners, but they were appropriately swept up in the enormity of what was before them. By the time they were finished—they didn't even make a dent, to be honest—their faces were almost totally smudged with sugar and happiness. But they got hold of themselves, wiped their faces clean with napkins that you don't throw away, and focused on the business at hand.

But before they could even launch into the questions, the leader leaned toward the kids and looked furtively from side to side like he was about to tell them a secret. In a whispered voice he said, "You know, when I was your age, my dad used to pretend that he had forgotten his hat in the woods and would send me to fetch it. Don't tell my soldiers this, but I was afraid that the bears were going to get me. So I would whistle like this . . ." He broke out into a whistled song for the children and he had them whistle along. Then, with the look of a sincere friend in a heavy Russian accent, he said to the kids, "This is my promise to you: I'll never let the bears get you."

And with that preamble, he shared his thoughts drenched in sincerity about how a friend knows what you need even before you ask. He ended his talk with these words that still ring true for our family.

"You know what it is about someone that makes them a friend? A friend doesn't just say things; a friend *does*."

••••◦━◆━◦••••

At the end of each interview, the kids thanked the leader for taking the time to meet as they handed over a small red box. Each leader carefully unwrapped their present, lifted the lid, and held up the key to our front door. The kids told each leader that they had really meant it about coming to our home and invited them to bring their keys when they came—you know, since they were friends now.

The prince loved his key, promised that he would make good use of it, and invited his new young friends to dinner at his house. This kind of invitation happened often because, even though the formal meetings were over, friendship creates a whole new economy. When people realize there's no agenda other than friendship and better understanding, it changes things. The leaders realized we weren't there to tell them to stop doing this, start doing that, or talk about controversies or conflicting beliefs or plans.

I want to live in a new normal where I can reach out to people who are different from me and just be friends. I remember hearing in elementary school that we could be pen pals with someone far away. That was great and all, but there's a big difference between being pen pals and being real pals. To make an impact you have to go there and start a friendship. Friends *do*—they don't just think about it.

When the kids returned from one of the trips, they read that Tun Mahathir, the prime minister of Malaysia and longest-serving leader in Asia, had hosted the world Islamic Conference. Mahathir drew significant criticism from the international community by saying the words in his keynote address "Death to America, and death to Israel." Our State Department condemned the comments, but the kids had a better idea. They had just met with the president of Israel and wanted to share his hopes with Tun Mahathir in another in-person meeting. They sent a letter and the next week, Mahathir's people cabled back that he would meet them just outside of Kuala Lumpur the following Wednesday. It's pretty short notice to fly around the world, but we figured, what the heck? So we sold the pickup truck and went! Because that's how love rolls; it does.

Something happens when you get engaged, doesn't it? It changes everything. And the friendships made during those early days by the kids continue to this day and have dramatically expanded. Why? Because they were authentic friendships; there were no angles, no plan in particular other than to be friends.

There was no agenda either; there was nothing on the other side of the equals sign to make it balance—just us. And it was all about whimsy, but it was a strategic whimsy on the kids' part, one that was wise beyond its years.

You'll never guess what happened a little while later. Lindsey opened up her e-mail and there was a short note from a leader from one of the countries. It didn't say much, just this: "Dear Lindsey, we miss you and your brothers. Can we please use our key and come over for a sleepover?"

And they did.

....

CHAPTER 11

THERE'S MORE ROOM

I used to think I needed an invitation to get into most places,
but now I know I'm already invited.

My friend Brandon and I were in Washington, DC, together taking care of a few things. One night, we were close to Capitol Hill and it was pretty late—almost midnight. We noticed a bunch of cars awkwardly parked around the Library of Congress. You would investigate, right? Yeah, us too. As we got closer, we saw a discreetly placed sign on the dashboard of one of the cars that was being used to barricade the Library. It read, "National Treasure 2."

It didn't take us long to make sense of the scene, and practically in unison we turned to each other and blurted, "No way!

They're filming *National Treasure 2* inside the Library of Congress *right now.*" We knew right then and there that our evening plans had changed—we were going to sneak onto the set.

We ran back to where we were staying, swapped our suits for blue jeans and shirts so we could look like part of the film crew, and rushed back to the Library. We had to dodge a couple of security guards, dash across a couple of lawns, and cut through some bushes, but a few minutes later, we found ourselves in the area where all the electrical cables and camera equipment were being unpacked. There was a side entrance for crew only, so we played the part and walked toward the door like we were supposed to be there. Nobody noticed us. People were passing us on the left and right, but nobody suspected a thing. We just kept acting like we belonged and walked farther and farther into the Library. At the end of each corridor there was a small sheet of paper taped to the wall with an arrow and the word "Set" printed on it. We were getting worried that this was so easy.

We rounded a corner and were immediately met by a metal detector and a guard. The burst of adrenaline I felt told me we were busted—this caper was going to end poorly, for sure, and I knew we would be in a lot of trouble for being in the Library of Congress in the middle of the night.

"Where are your crew badges?" the security guard barked at us while talking to his girlfriend on his cell phone.

"We don't have them," we said kind of pathetically.

He mumbled something to his girlfriend about guys like us on the film crew and shook his head. Irritated, he waved us through the metal detector. We moved through and sprinted down the hall while the guard was shouting something about "badges . . . next time."

We turned the last corner and made it to the set. We were standing in the Library of Congress and it was two o'clock in the morning. The building is massive and ornate and holds hundreds of thousands of books. Millions of books. Every book, supposedly. I wondered how the members of Congress had time to read all these.

There was a somber silence underneath the grand dome. And it was *hot*. The movie lights were on, and, having since seen the movie, I think they were filming the scene where the actors are looking for the *Presidential Book of Secrets*. It's a pretty cool scene. We could have powered the lights with our nervous energy. Mostly because of all of the Capitol police and security guards surrounding the set. It's one thing to walk onto the set like you know what you're doing. But once you get there, everybody has a job and looks busy. It's not like we could grab a camera and start filming. So after a short while, once we knew we had a great story to tell the next day, we started whispering to each other, "How are we going to get out of here without getting caught?" Now is when I should cue the intense movie score.

Just when Brandon and I were about to turn on our heels to get out, Nicolas Cage rounded the corner in a tuxedo along with lead actress Diane Kruger in her gown. We moved out of the way as they walked by and, without even talking, fell in behind them like we belonged in their entourage. No kidding. We walked past cast, crew, and security as well as the Capitol Hill police. Nobody even asked us a question. We followed the actors right out the front door, and when they turned to the right to head toward their trailers with stars on them, we turned to the left to head into some bushes with leaves on them.

·••●◀▮▶●••·

My brief cameo on the *National Treasure 2* set was not my first time in DC. The Goff family has been to the White House many times. Not officially or anything, just to visit and see the nice paintings and guys with guns under their jackets talking into their sleeves. Our visits always seemed to be around Easter because there would be this swanky Easter egg hunt happening on the lawn. We never got invited to that event, but Sweet Maria and I had a fun idea for the kids. We'd show up Easter morning and hide eggs along the black metal fence that separates those on the "inside" from the rest of us. We would dress up and everything to pretend like we were part of the distinguished gathering. I was always tempted to roll one of our eggs under the fence so the guys with suits and earpieces would tackle us and then talk into their sleeves.

Our little strip of grass on the sidewalk of Pennsylvania Avenue was modest in comparison to the beautifully manicured Rose Garden. With such a small area to work with, our eggs were super easy to spot. The kids were young enough that they really didn't notice the lack of hiding places. They just figured they were really good at finding Easter eggs, I guess. I've always wanted my kids to know that they were included in important things, that they belonged there, that they were invited.

There are lots of things in life you and I don't get invited to, though. I've never been invited to the Oscars or to Paul McCartney's birthday party or to a space shuttle launch. I'm waiting for my invitation to *National Treasure 3*. If I got an invitation to any of those things, or for that matter, to the real White House Easter egg hunt, I'd definitely go. There's nothing like feeling included.

There is only one invitation it would kill me to refuse, yet I'm tempted to turn it down all the time. I get the invitation every morning when I wake up to actually live a life of complete engagement, a life of whimsy, a life where love does. It doesn't come in an envelope. It's ushered in by a sunrise, the sound of a bird, or the smell of coffee drifting lazily from the kitchen. It's the invitation to actually live, to fully participate in this amazing life for one more day. Nobody turns down an invitation to the White House, but I've seen plenty of people turn down an invitation to fully live.

Turning down this invitation comes in lots of flavors. It looks like numbing yourself or distracting yourself or seeing something really beautiful as just normal. It can also look like refusing to forgive or not being grateful or getting wrapped around the axle with fear or envy. I think every day God sends us an invitation to live and sometimes we forget to show up or get head-faked into thinking we haven't really been invited. But you see, we have been invited—every day, all over again.

There's no doubt Jesus invites us to have some very cool experiences in our lives, and for that matter, in the afterlife. Jesus tells a story in the Bible about a rich guy who had a banquet. The rich guy invited lots of people, but most of them made excuses and didn't come, so the guy sent his servants to invite other folks—but this time he invited the unlikely ones, people who normally don't get invited to anything, folks like me. The message he had for this new round of people was simple: "There's more room." That was it. It wasn't a deep theological treatise. Yet it was exactly that, deep and theological. I think life is like that banquet Jesus talked about. I think God sends out His messengers to tell everybody there's plenty of room and there's free food and conversation and adventure and a wonderful and generous host who has invited us by name.

It's as though the people invited to the White House Easter egg hunt don't bother to show, and the president sends out the guys in the suits to see if anybody else wants to come. Maybe people like us who were just on the other side of the fence. The servants come up to each of us, lean in close, and whisper in our ears, "There's more room." That's it. That's all that needs to be said. There aren't any magic words to say in response, and we don't need to give a speech or get a bracelet or a bumper sticker or a tattoo. We just need to decide to be fully engaged. In that way, life can be like a sweepstakes, one where you must be present to win.

I don't think God is the kind of guy who forces Himself on anybody either. If people don't want to come to the banquet, He's not bitter or anything. He loves them all the same, but He's not going to force them. Instead, He just keeps looking. He keeps saying there's more room to those who really want to be invited to where He is. He's like any of us in that way. I think God pays attention to our hearts and enjoys when people want to get close to Him. He knows our sadness and the brokenness we want to hide from Him, and He sends people to look for us.

When I was young and thought about God and church and Jesus, I would shy away because I thought getting close to God was like breaking onto the set of *National Treasure 2*. I thought there were lots of long corridors to navigate, there were arrows pointing in all kinds of directions, and the religious people were the security guards. They were the people checking to see if you had been invited. But Jesus never acted like that. When you read the Bible, the people who loved Jesus and followed Him were the ones like me who don't get invited places. Yet Jesus told His friends they were invited anyway. In fact, He told them that the religious people weren't the ones who decided who got into heaven and who didn't. He said the people who followed Him should think of themselves more like the ushers rather than the bouncers, and it would be God who decides who gets in. We're the ones who simply show people their seats that someone else paid for.

Can you even believe that Jesus would invite people to a banquet and they wouldn't want to show up? When we accept Jesus' invitation to show up to life, we get to do life with Him, and He's way more powerful and important than the president. Or Nicolas Cage.

A couple of other things happen when we accept Jesus' invitation to participate with Him in life. Obstacles that seem insurmountable aren't. Impediments that we believe disqualify us don't. When we show up to participate with Jesus in the big life, we're participating with the very being who made life in the first place. He gently asks us how we are and invites us to get better together with Him.

Accepting the invitation to show up in life is about moving from the bleachers to the field. It's moving from developing opinions to developing options. It's about having things matter to us enough that we stop just thinking about those things and actually *do* something about them. Simply put, Jesus is looking for us to accept the invitation to participate. It's like the president is calling and we just need to answer the phone. We need to show up.

When we accept life's invitation, it's contagious too. Other people will watch us and start seeing life as something more amazing, more whimsical than before. When you show up to the big life, people (the type who don't think they're invited) start seeing invitations everywhere as thick as colorful fall leaves. They don't think about their pain or their weakness any longer. Instead, they think about how incredible a big life really is and how powerful the one who is throwing the banquet is too.

Jesus wants us to come. He's sending His servants out to tell the people standing at the fences and in the libraries that they're invited to the party. He's sending you an invitation too, in the sunrise, in the sound of a bird, or in the smell of coffee drifting lazily from the kitchen. The one who has invited you is way more powerful than any of the impediments we think we're facing, and He has just one message for us. He leans forward and whispers quietly to each of us, "There's more room."

CHAPTER 12

....

WOW, WHAT A HIT!

I used to think the words spoken about us describe who we are,
but now I know they shape who we are.

When I was in elementary school, I played Little League baseball. I wasn't much of a sports guy. I suppose I was okay, except for the catching and throwing and hitting aspects of the game. I had a uniform, a cap, a glove, and baseball cards in the spokes of my bicycle, so the coach let me on the team and put me out in right field where very little happens. When you're that young, nobody hits the ball to right field.

I was bigger than any of the other guys on the team, so everybody assumed I could hit. The fact was, I couldn't. Because I was such a big guy, I almost covered the plate. I wasn't afraid of the ball and the pitchers weren't very accurate, so part of our team's strategy was to send me to the plate to get beaned by a pitch or two each inning. In baseball, when you get hit, you get sent to first base and you don't even need to swing the bat. I think baseball is the only game where all you need to do is take a ball in the face and you win.

My sad, sad batting average was the result of this one bad fundamental: every time I swung the bat, I closed my eyes. It was as if my eyes and my arms were connected somehow. All season long, the only way I got on base was by getting hit. By the end of the season, I also had seventeen bone-deep bruises and a concussion.

Somehow, our team got to the playoffs. I had very little to do with it, of course, apart from the bruises and a few loose teeth. Regardless, we were in. In the first playoff game, it was tied in the top of the fifth inning, and it was my turn to bat. I could hear the stands groan at the sight of the big kid who couldn't hit the ball walking up to the plate. I heard a chant starting from our own bleachers, "Hit him . . . hit him . . . hit him," hoping I'd get nailed again by the pitcher and take a base. I tried to put aside the possibility that my dad might be leading the chant.

The pitcher missed me with the first couple of tosses, and suddenly I had two strikes. I wanted to end my season with a blaze of glory, so I clinched my teeth, tightened my grip, and decided to go down swinging. (Feel free to read the next couple of lines in slow motion.) The last pitch came soaring from the mound; I closed my eyes and swung as hard as I could. I heard this dull *thwap* and felt a new sensation in my hands. Somehow, miraculously, I had connected with the ball. I was so startled at first that I just stood there. Then someone on the bench shouted, "Run!"—so like Forrest Gump, I ran.

I galumphed around first base and watched as the ball sailed out into center field, bounced off the top of the fence, and fell over on the home run side. As I rounded third, I soaked in my glory as I stampeded toward home plate, arms raised high, making a referee's signal for a touchdown because I didn't know the difference.

In the end, the other team scored about a dozen more runs in the next couple of innings and we lost miserably. But I hardly noticed because my home run was playing over and over in my mind. It was a slow-motion loop in my imagination with different camera angles and lots of old-fashioned camera bulbs flashing, people cheering or pointing upward toward the ball or dropping their popcorn or sodas as they sprang to their feet to see what I'd just done. Everyone looked amazed, me most of all.

A week or so later, I was in my room and my mom told me I had some mail. *Mail? For me?* I opened the big envelope and inside was a card. I think that it was the first card I'd ever received in the mail, and it was shaped like an apple. I wondered if all cards were shaped like apples. When I opened the card, the words "You are the apple of my eye" had been printed by Hallmark inside. In handwriting below were the words "Wow . . . What a hit, Bob! You're a real ball player. Love, Coach."

I reread the words over and over. "Wow . . . What a hit!" I thought, *It really wasn't that great of a hit. Did he know my eyes were closed?* I read it again, "Wow . . . What a hit!" I thought about the dozens of times I had struck out or just stepped in front of the ball hoping my current black eye could heal before I got a new one. Then I read it again, "Wow . . . What a hit!" What about all the times I had dropped the ball or threw it into the stands by mistake? It didn't matter. "Wow . . . What a hit! I'm a real ball player," I read out loud to myself. And not only that, I was the apple of his eye.

I heard a self-help guy say once you could look in the mirror and give yourself something he called positive affirmations, like saying to yourself you are good or smart or talented. I don't know if that works, to be honest. Maybe it does. But I do know one thing that works every time—it's having somebody else say something good about you. I think that's how we were created, you know, to get named by people this way. I think God speaks something meaningful into our lives and it fills us up and helps us change the world regardless of ourselves and our shortcomings. His name for us is His beloved. He hopes that we'll believe Him like I came to believe what the coach said about me. He hopes we'll start to see ourselves as His beloved rather than think of all of the reasons that we aren't.

Sometimes we don't think that the name someone picked for us is accurate either. How could the coach think of me as a real ball player? And how could God think of me as His beloved? But then I remember Jesus said to one of the guys with Him that he was a rock even though He knew this same guy would deny ever knowing Him. I don't think Jesus was blowing sunshine at Peter when He did that. Instead, I think He was calling something out from inside Peter. It was kind of like the coach telling me I was a real ball player—he saw it in me and was just calling it out. We get to do that for each other still today.

It's over forty years later and I've watched a few baseball games, but not many. I don't have reason to think about Little League or elementary school days often. But when I do, I still think about that card from my coach. And in my mind I can see myself pulling it out of the envelope. I can see that it's shaped like an apple and inside, the words from a kind man—"You're the apple of my eye. Wow . . . What a hit, Bob! You're a real ball player. Love, Coach."

Words of encouragement are like that. They have their own power. And when they are said by the right people, they can change everything. What I've found in following Jesus is that most of the time, when it comes to who says it, we each are the right people. And I've concluded something else. That the words people say to us not only have shelf life but have the ability to shape life.

....

CHAPTER 13

BIGGER AND BETTER

I used to think I needed to sacrifice for God,
but now I know faith is like a game of Bigger and Better.

W hen I was a kid we used to play a game called Bigger and Better. You probably played the same game when you were young too. In this game, everybody starts with something of little value, like a dime, and then everybody heads out into the neighborhood to see what they can it trade for. You knock on people's doors and ask if they'd be willing to trade something for the dime, and then you go to the next door with whatever they traded you. The goal is to come back with a bigger, better thing than you started out with. The bigger it is, the better it is.

My son Richard set out with a dime awhile back. He went to the first door and said, "Hi, we're playing Bigger and Better. I've got a dime, and I'm hoping to trade up to something bigger. Do you have anything you can trade me?" The guy at the door had never heard of this game. Nevertheless, he was immediately in and he shouted over his shoulder to his wife, "Hey, Marge, there's a kid here and *we're* playing Bigger and Better." (I love that he said "we.") "What do we have that's bigger and better than a dime?" Richard walked away with a mattress.

Rich went with his buddies to the next door and they knocked while Rich stood on the porch with his mattress. The door opened and his muffled voice could barely be heard as he shouted through the Serta pillow top asking if this next neighbor would trade with him for something bigger and better than a mattress. A little while later, he skipped away from the house having traded the mattress for a Ping-Pong table.

Richard wheeled the Ping-Pong table to the next house and traded up for an elk head. How cool is that? I would have stopped there, but Rich didn't. He kept trading up. By the end of the night, when Rich came home, he didn't have a dime or a mattress, a Ping-Pong table or an elk head, or the five other things he traded up. Richard drove home in a pickup truck. No lie. He started with a dime and ended up with a Dodge.

I remember reading this quote from C. S. Lewis where he says, "It would seem that Our Lord finds our desires not too strong, but too weak. We are half-hearted creatures, fooling about with drink and sex and ambition when infinite joy is offered us, like an ignorant child who wants to go on making mud pies in a slum because he cannot imagine what is meant by the offer of a holiday at the sea. We are far too easily pleased."

That quote reminds me of a passage in the Bible about a young guy who had a lot of money. He was a good guy, very religious, kept the commandments and the whole bit. Jesus told this upstanding guy that if he really wanted to know God, he needed to sell all his possessions and follow Him. The man was sad about the exchange. Like me, he liked his stuff, but he liked Jesus too. Ultimately, though, that young man decided he'd worked too hard for what he had, whatever he had to trade to get to Jesus was just too important, and what Jesus had to offer was just too intangible. So he chose to keep his stuff rather than follow Jesus.

Jesus doesn't have this conversation to shame the rich young ruler. The challenge that comes into sharp relief is whether we are willing to give up all we have to follow Him, to know God. Are we willing to trade up? It's a question worth asking because the answer will shape your life one way or the other.

We've all given up something at one time or another. At first, it always feels like a huge sacrifice to give up what we've got. To Jesus, though, it's no sacrifice at all. Think about it from His perspective. He comes from heaven, where He has an amazing love relationship with the Father, which, by its nature, is the most beautiful existence any person could have. And He offers that to anybody willing to let go of whatever is giving them a false sense of security. Why would anybody not make that trade? Jesus is basically saying, "Look, none of the stuff you have is going to last, including you. You've only got about a dime's worth of life now. Come and trade up, come follow Me, and you can know God." In that sense, Jesus isn't requesting a sacrifice at all. He's asking us to play Bigger and Better, where we give up ourselves and end up with Him.

It's important to note here that Jesus didn't ask everybody

to give up all their stuff. This is something He asked of the rich young ruler because He wanted to teach the young man that he wasn't as holy as he thought he was. He wanted to teach the young man that he still needed God's help, to look at what he had and decide whether he would rather have that, or trade up and have what Jesus is offering: a life with Him.

Actually, the real game of Bigger and Better that Jesus is playing with us usually isn't about money or possessions or even our hopes. It's about our pride. He asks if we'll give up that thing we're so proud of, that thing we believe causes us to *matter* in the eyes of the world, and give it up to follow Him. He's asking us, "Will you take what you think defines you, leave it behind, and let Me define who you are instead?"

The cool thing about taking Jesus up on His offer is that whatever controls you doesn't anymore. People who used to be obsessed about becoming famous no longer care whether anybody knows their name. People who used to want power are willing to serve. People who used to chase money freely give it away. People who used to beg others for acceptance are now strong enough to give love.

When we get our security from Christ, we no longer have to look for it in the world, and that's a pretty good trade.

Do you know what Rich did with that truck? He gave it away. He drove it to a church down the street and tossed them the keys. He didn't need it and didn't want it and what he got in exchange for it was bigger and better still. He got a sense of satisfaction, confidence, and reaffirmation that stuff didn't have control over him. While it was a good story to have traded up and gotten a truck, it was an even better story, a more whimsical one, to have given it away in the end. And he got to serve God, not by sacrificing, but by trading up in the way he lives his life. Although he started with just a dime, he walked away with a great example of how Jesus sees us in the world.

Religious people say that Jesus stands at the door and knocks. I agree. But there's more. Jesus invites us to stand at the door of His house and do some knocking too. And when He opens a door, He wants us to bring all of the faith we have to Him, even if it's just a dime's worth. And He promises that He will trade up with us—because He Himself is what we have the chance to trade for. And what we'll have to give in exchange for knowing Him is everything we've accumulated during our lives and are standing on the porch holding on to.

....

CHAPTER 14

A NEW KIND OF DIET

I used to think religion tasted horrible,
but now I know I was just eating the fake stuff.

A couple of buddies and I decided to lose a little weight this year. These are guys who will give you lots of trouble if you don't follow through, and there's no way I wanted to be the last guy dropping pounds, so I changed a few of my habits.

On the first morning, I stood in front of the refrigerator with the door wide open like my teenage boys do, as though they are watching a movie—a very cold and expensive movie. I reached for a bagel and some Philadelphia cream cheese in the familiar silver-wrapped package. This is not the breakfast choice of a love-handle-shedding champion, but I spread it a little thinner than usual and thought maybe I'd lose a few ounces anyway.

Our family friend Ashley was staying at our house and must have bought the low-fat cream cheese this time, I thought as I cut a chunk out of the wrapper and spread it like a veneer on the bagel. I took a bite and it tasted terrible. I honestly couldn't believe anybody ate this low-fat junk. I thought, *Maybe if I put more of the fake cream cheese on my bagel it might taste a little more like the real thing.* So I cut a bigger chunk out of the bar and spread it on thick. I took another bite, but no difference. It actually tasted worse.

I took the second half of the bagel and decided I'd go no-nonsense on it too. *What the heck. If this stuff is half the calories, I can use twice as much,* I reasoned. I cut another couple of big chunks out of the cream cheese, leaving just enough so I could put it back in the refrigerator with dignity. There was no salvaging this healthy substitute. Every bite was as awful as the last.

Sweet Maria came into the kitchen as I finished force-feeding myself this lackluster breakfast.

"Hey," I said, "will you please tell Ashley not to get this low-fat junk anymore? It's *horrible.*"

"Sure, I guess," she said with a quizzical look on her face.

Then she walked over to the near-empty package, inspected it, and started belly-laughing.

"What?" I said, confused.

In a satisfying tone, the kind that revels in moments like this, she explained that I had just eaten nearly a whole bar of Crisco lard.

Around the house, we call that being "head-faked." It's a sports term, I guess, but we say it when we thought things were one way but we got duped and it turns out that they are entirely different. Unfortunately, it happens to me in life all the time, and in faith too. It's the stuff that masquerades as the real thing but it's not. The perplexing thing is, instead of putting the fake stuff down, our reaction is usually to put more fake stuff on or decide the fake stuff, while not that good, is good enough.

If you ask a thousand people who don't want anything to do with religion why that is, they'll tell you all the reasons they don't like it, but I doubt they'd be describing the real stuff. They'll describe a guy or a gal on a television show who told them if they gave money, they'd get rich. They'll talk about the big hairdo or outrageous makeup of some televangelist and the absurd things they said and did. They'll talk about someone who was religious but broke their hearts or their promise, or lied and got caught or went to jail, or who cried a lot on camera but it looked like they were faking it. Or they'll talk about someone who told them that God hated who they were or how they acted or who they married or couldn't forgive what they'd done. It's a sad situation, honestly. The only way they can keep from being head-faked anymore is for somebody to give them a taste of the real thing. And what's great is that we each have a shot at being that person.

In the Bible there's a guy named Timothy who gets a letter from another guy named Paul. Paul is like an older brother to Timothy. In the letter, Paul tells him to watch out for people who act holy but don't get their holiness from Jesus but from the stuff they've done, which is pure delusion. Paul called this kind of religious devotion a form of godlessness, meaning it's the exact opposite of what it's pretending to be. He was telling Timothy to watch out for people who fake it with their faith. In other words, some religion looks like it's wrapped in the right package, but it's actually Crisco.

There are a couple of examples in the Bible of folks who were faking it. Jesus usually used lawyers and religious people as examples for what He didn't like, and that hits pretty close to home for me. One religious guy named Sceva had seven sons. They were talking about Jesus, but it turns out that they were full of Crisco and one of the bad guys they met called them on it. He said, "I know who Jesus is, and I know who Paul is . . . but who are you?"

Like Sceva's sons, it seems like a lot of people who say they know Jesus have all the right words and all the right moves, but what they don't have is sincerity and authenticity. They talk a big game and use a bunch of twenty-pound words to describe an otherwise simple idea about faith. But in reality, they never really do anything. It's like a guy with a cowboy hat, one duck, one cow, and a tractor calling himself a rancher. We don't want to be all hat and no cattle when it comes to faith.

The Bible story about Sceva's sons ends with them getting their butts kicked. Not my words, the Bible's. God doesn't like it when people fake it. It's the same as identity theft in a way, only the fakers are stealing God's identity and using it to make people feel bad or force them to change who they are to fit into a particular religious community. You can usually tell when someone is doing this because, just like Sceva's sons, they use Jesus' name a lot, but it doesn't seem that they have any of the power Jesus said would come with knowing Him. That power is easy to spot because it usually comes in the form of grace and acceptance, as well as sincere love and respect. It's the kind of power that actually does things rather than just talking about them.

More often than I'd like to admit, I find myself saying or doing things, calculating how it will make me sound or look to others. For example, I say that I don't have the time to do something when what I really lack is compassion. Jesus is asking me and the rest of the people in the world to stop faking it. He wants us to fight the temptation to merely have the right wrapper and instead be exactly who He made us to be and who we are right where we are.

None of us want to make God look bad. But in the end, being fake makes God look worse. It makes people think He tastes like Crisco.

Not only that, but when we meet people who have been fed the fake stuff about who God is and what He's about, it's not surprising that they have a little indigestion. So we can either spend our time talking about wrappers or we can show them what God is really made of. We can show them that God is full of love and is the source of hope and every creative idea. People don't want to be told that their experiences were wrong or that their wrapper or someone else's wrapper is made of the wrong stuff. Instead, we get to be the ones to show them real love from a real God.

I'm more careful about what I grab now when I go to the refrigerator. I'm a little afraid that I'll end up with another bagel full of lard, or perhaps worse. But if it does happen again, I'm not going to fake it or take another bite, and I won't put it back in the wrapper for the next person. I'm going to put it down, walk away slowly, and grab something that's better for me. Maybe an apple, although people have had problems in the past with those too.

CHAPTER 15

....

A WORD NOT TO USE

I used to think words were all the same,
but now I know there are some words I shouldn't use.

D on is a friend of mine. He's written a bunch of books. It seems that just about everyone knows him, and he's sold probably a couple million copies of his books, maybe more. He'd never tell me, and I'd feel lame asking, so I haven't. Don is one of those secretly incredible guys who doesn't talk about what he's going to do. He just does stuff—not to direct attention to himself but to point people toward an approachable God. Don actually played a big part in this book. He would review what I wrote and tell me to keep working on it or take it out of the book. Sometimes he'd tell me to start over entirely or tell me what to do to make it better.

Don would say, "Hey, Bob, I think *our* writing will be better if *we could . . .*" and then he'd tell me what to change. I would tease Don and tell him that I'm happy I can help this *New York Times* best-selling author with "our" writing.

One day Don said I shouldn't use the word *that*.

"Really? What's wrong with writing 'that'?" I asked.

He didn't explain—he just said I wasn't supposed to use it. And he said it like he knew. He said I should treat the word *that* like it's a cuss word.

"A cuss word? Really? How come?"

I know a couple of cuss words, and "that" isn't one of them.

I never really got an answer to this question. And I suppose it's proper grammar to use it here and there, but not often. But none of it matters to me. All I know is Don is a great writer and he said *our* writing would be better if *we* didn't use the word *that*. So now I avoid using it. I'm still not 100 percent sure why, but I trust Don and that's enough.

I think faith can be kind of the same because Jesus didn't always *explain* everything in great detail. If someone I trust tells me something, and I know it's for my benefit, I just trust it. I'm fine with the possibility someone might be wrong, particularly when I weigh they might be right and my life would be better if I did what they suggest. Remember, though, I'm a lawyer. I deal with sneaky people for a living, so I'm no pushover. I've learned to sharpen my intuition about *why* someone offers me input. I've found one of the best filters you can use to trust someone is when there's nothing for them to gain from their advice.

Here's what I mean. Many people have angles attached to their relationships. They will say or do one thing and you learn later they were actually angling for something else in return.

We've all experienced this. A lot of Christians do the same thing with their faith without really noticing it. It's not because they're malicious or anything. They've just bought into the hype that faith is like an exclusive club you're in. They take what used to be authentic friendships and use them like a networking cocktail mixer. They call what the rest of us call normal acts of kindness "ministry" or go on a wonderful adventure to see another country and call it a "mission trip." It can come across as formulaic and manipulative to toss out some buzz words and slip past the bouncers into the club. But these folks run the risk of downgrading a genuine and sincere faith into an infomercial for God or their own status.

What I like about Jesus is that He didn't try to recruit people or use spin. Neither He nor His disciples ever said they were going on a mission trip, because they weren't. He just invited everyone and said they could follow Him. He didn't use big words or Christian code to cue people that He was in the club or that He wanted to protect His reputation. Or talk about all of the things He was going to do or the number of people He was going to have "pray the prayer" to accept Him. He didn't present God's plan like a prospectus promising a return on investment. He just asked people to join the adventure. It's almost like Jesus came to say, among other things, that a relationship with Him isn't supposed to make complete sense or provide security. Faith isn't an equation or a formula or a business deal that gets you what you want. In short, there's nothing on the other side of the equals sign, just Jesus.

Jesus didn't give people a lot of directions about what they should and shouldn't say either. But He did talk quite a bit about their hearts. He said their hearts would be better if they stayed away from certain things. It was kind of like He told them not to write the word *that* into their lives. Not because He was trying to control their lives, but because He wanted them to write their lives better, I suppose. I trust Don because he's a good author. I trust God because He's the best author. I think God doesn't spell out everything for us in life, but He does tell us how we can write our lives better; and trusting Him implicitly is always the right place to start.

My favorite book isn't *War and Peace* or *Huckleberry Finn*, although *Huckleberry Finn* is close. It's a thesaurus. The reason is simple. There are hundreds of words, probably thousands of them listed that can capture an idea or thought and propose words to describe those thoughts or ideas with greater precision, which would add much more clarity to what I'm trying to say. Now I try to explain my faith in much the same way a thesaurus does and see if I can't swap a word that is used far too much for another that might add more meaning, more life. I still don't know why Don told me not to write the word *that*, but I'd like to think it has something to do with how he wants me to stretch for a better, clearer way to express myself than I have done in the past. I think God maybe feels the same way.

....

CHAPTER 16

HUNTING GRIZZLIES

*I used to think I had missed the mark and God was mad about it,
but now I know "missing the mark" is a stupid analogy.*

When I was a kid, I had a great relationship with my dad, and my dad loved guns. My sister and I didn't get along that well—she was bigger than I was and beat me up—so I would mostly hang out with my mom or dad. Back then, my dad either spent his time gardening or doing something that revolved around hunting. He had a huge rifle and treated it like a classic car, rubbing it with oils and soft cloths. When my dad was done pampering the rifle, he would let me hold it and we'd pretend I was out on the trail of a grizzly bear. I was about eight years old and hadn't actually ever seen a grizzly bear, but I could imagine it perfectly in my mind, hiding behind the couch or under the dining room table.

My dad patiently taught me how to handle and shoot a rifle. He taught me a healthy respect for guns, about how dangerous they were and how carefully they had to be treated. I was his young apprentice.

"Son, you need to look through the scope at the things that are far away, but you also need to take your eye away long enough to see what's close." The life lessons in that statement escaped me at the time, but I've come back to words of wisdom like this when I was about to pull the trigger on a trial or a business deal or a caper of some sort.

"Then," he would continue with the seriousness of a monk, "it's all about how you pull the trigger." He was almost at a whisper as he continued, "If you pull hard, it will jerk the gun off target. So you need to pull the trigger super slow."

I stared back at him, my eyes glued to his. "Got it, Dad. Super slow."

"What you do is this . . ." He leaned forward and wrapped his arms around mine while I held the rifle. "You take a full breath." He breathed in deeply. "You let half of it out . . . then slowly squeeze the trigger." He almost chanted it like a poem. "Take a full breath . . . let half of it out . . . then slowly squeeze the trigger." He repeated it over and over, so I did too. I didn't want to forget. Not with grizzlies loose in the house.

My mom was not enthusiastic about guns, but my dad insisted they were safe when treated with respect. He would also go off on tangents about how guns were mentioned in the Constitution, and the way I remember it, it was our responsibility as Americans to own them, and Americans are supposed to train their children to use guns so they can shoot the British if they try that invasion thing again. So, against her better judgment, my mom let Dad keep a couple of guns in the house.

My dad was so serious about guns he even made his own ammo. Not the ammo like in the Revolutionary War, like musket balls, but actual modern-looking, pointier ammo you could shoot a grizzly bear with. The polished brass shell casings might as well have been gold coins in his hand, and my dad would sit in a chair by the window filling the casings with gunpowder he pulled from a small bag at his feet. Don't get the impression that we lived on Ruby Ridge or were survivalists or anything. My dad simply loved making ammo—like some people love making bread.

After a long and loving process, in order to make sure the bullet wouldn't jam in the rifle, my dad would run the shell through the gun. During all this, he kept his rifle leaning against the table, and after running a bullet through, he would tuck it into a box with the others. They stood like a row of soldiers ready to take the field.

My favorite part about my dad's rifle was the big, dark telescopic scope. The scope was huge, manly, and looked like it came right out of a sniper movie. And it even had crosshairs. Guys like anything with crosshairs. That's why guys don't watch romantic movies, because there aren't any crosshairs. If they released a *Pride and Prejudice* with crosshairs over some of the characters, guys would line up for days to take their girlfriends.

One day, when I got a little older, my dad was making his bullets and I asked if I could hunt the grizzly. He considered my request quietly and thoughtfully, then he checked the chamber of the gun to make sure it wasn't carrying any live ammunition.

He leaned it in my direction, and I gripped it slowly like I was being sworn into the Secret Service. I lifted it off the ground, swung it around carefully, and put my eye against the scope, looking through the crosshairs for the grizzly. We needed a new rug in front of the fireplace, and this might be our chance. Looking through that scope, I was no longer standing in the den with my dad. I was crouched in a dark forest dressed in full camouflage waiting for the grizzly to walk through the room. And then one did.

With the glass of the scope against my eye, I silently recited the words my dad taught me. I took a full breath, let half of it out, and then I slowly squeezed the trigger.

Turns out, there was a bullet in the gun.

The violent sound that ripped through our house sounded like a cannon blast.

The bullet cut through the air at eighteen hundred feet per second, drilling its way through the sheetrock and boring through bracing studs like butter. It buzzed through the hallway and into the next room, where it lodged itself just over my sister's bed.

Because of the way I was holding the rifle with the stock tucked under my arm and the scope firmly against my eye, I took the full recoil around my right eye. After a couple of minutes, I came to and noticed my favorite T-shirt was drenched in blood. My first thought was that I had done something wrong, and I was going to get spanked. My second thought was about whether I got the grizzly. A neighborhood boy who had been over playing ran outside to tell all the neighbors I had just shot myself in the head. My sister ran in the house to ask if she could have my bike.

Through my bloody eye I could see my dad standing over me, distraught but determined. He scooped me into his arms and got blood all over his shirt. He carried me away to the hospital, and the doctors stitched me up. I was sent home black and blue but looking very manly. My sister gave me a disappointed look when she realized I was still alive and she wouldn't be getting my bike. I walked into her room, stared at the bullet hole, and calculated the distance between it and her pillow. "Just down and to the right," I said. She never picked on me again after that.

····◆····

I tell you that story because much later I'd meet some Christians who used gun analogies about targets and missing the mark and all that. Or maybe it was about archery. Nevertheless, this analogy would be dragged out to tell us we were all blowing it and falling short. They also talked about how God was really mad at certain people because of what they believed or about the things they'd done. These Christians sounded a little judgmental, to be honest. Looking back, though, these folks seemed dead-set on pulling the trigger more than anyone else I had met. They would find anybody who messed up or made a bad decision and get them in their sights.

I didn't like that, because I messed up a lot, and there's something creepy about feeling like you are in someone's crosshairs. Maybe it's one of those times where, like my dad said, these folks needed to take their eyes away from the scope for a while in order to see what's close, like their own hurts and mistakes. I think we all need to do that from time to time. I sure do.

As I've grown older, I've come to learn most people aren't bad in the traditional sense. I mean, they aren't malicious or plotting a bank robbery or setting up scams. The people I know, they are mostly aiming their crosshairs at stuff like being loved, not being lonely, finding some security, and a bunch of other things that are actually pretty normal and worth pursuing. In fact, I think God put it in our hearts to aim for those things, and it's nice when we actually hit those targets.

Sometimes, though, things can go horribly wrong and we end up flat on our backs in a blood-soaked T-shirt. I don't think God is mad at us when that happens. He knew when He made the world that there was going to be some pain and people were going to get hurt—whether they did it to themselves or others did it to them. He knew people were going to manipulate each other and cheat and try to get love and respect in inappropriate ways. Still, it's hard for me to see Him enjoying the pain when we fail.

These days, the view of God I hold on to isn't Him being mad because I've missed the mark. It's the one of Him seen through a bloody eye, scooping me into His arms, getting blood all over His shirt, and carrying me away to get healed.

....

CHAPTER 17

CORNER STORE ECONOMICS

I used to think rules were made by someone else,
but now I know we get to make some of our own.

When I was a kid, I used to walk to the corner store to buy candy. The store in our town had a bell on a spring that would jingle whenever the door opened. Inside was a wonderful old man at the register who was covered in gray hair and looked like the guy in the movie *Up*. He had white whiskers that poked out of his face like small cornstalks, and whenever someone entered and the bell rang, he'd stop bagging groceries to offer a grin and a nod. In my young mind, he was the candy keeper, the luckiest man in the whole world. I reasoned that anytime he wanted he could take a piece of candy, and he didn't even have to pay.

But I did have to pay, so all week, when my dad came home from work, I'd check his trouser pockets for loose change. When it looked like I might have enough, I'd walk down to the store. The bell would ring, and the old man would grin and nod, and I'd pace up and down the aisles like a curator at an art museum figuring out what candy acquisition I would make with my pocket change.

I'd take my choice to the register and spread my change on the counter. I never knew if I had enough, so I'd look the old man in the eye to learn if I had the right number of pennies and nickels. He would smile and in a low, gentle voice slowly count my hoard. I remember that his vest always smelled like pipe tobacco as he would lean onto the counter between jars and stacks of paper bags and move my change around like a banker.

When he counted to the right number, he'd slide the candy bar my way, scoop up the part of the money that was his, and give the rest back to me. I usually didn't wait to get home before eating the candy either. I'd stay in the company of the storekeeper and watch him bag groceries for whoever else came in. I liked listening to the small talk, predictions about the weather, or the happenings in town. The topic of conversation wasn't important—it was just the kind of place where you wanted to linger. The storekeeper would hear the same small-town gossip over and over every day, but each time he'd listen and respond as though each customer were sharing the news for the first time.

One morning, after having collected enough change from my dad, I ambled down to the store, chose my candy bar, and sprinkled my change before the storekeeper like a pirate's bounty. He began his usual process, separating the coins into rows like he always did. He counted in his gentle voice, stopping to remind me what each coin was worth. He asked me to count out loud with him. I usually stopped counting after eleven or twelve and he would finish up for us without making me feel bad. Somehow he made it sound like we were both still counting. When he was done, I'd look into his eyes to see if I had enough. He'd usually give me half a nod and a small grin to let me know I did. On this morning, though, things were different. When he finished counting, he shook his whiskered face and squinted. It was the first time this had happened, and I supposed this meant I didn't have enough.

"We're one penny short," he said sympathetically. When you're a kid, one penny is an impassable divide, and you can feel really alone when it's just you. But he said "we" and it made me feel like we were in this thing together, that my goal was his.

"I've got an idea," the storekeeper said after a couple of long moments. He grabbed one of the pennies as he reached behind the counter for an old rag and a bottle of vinegar. He poured a little vinegar over the rag and put a pinch of salt on it.

"I know exactly what you feel like." He grinned as he started rubbing the penny. "I know what it feels like to really want something and come up short." This was the longest sentence he had ever said to me.

"I really love watching over this store," he went on while I eyed the coin like it was part of a magic trick. "And I love that you come to see me so much." It felt like I was in some rite of passage—I was the one making small talk with the storekeeper now. I thought I'd mimic other conversations and bring up the weather, but he jumped in with a statement that changed everything.

As he finished rubbing the penny, it was a brilliant copper color, like it had been freshly minted. He dropped it onto the counter with the others and said, "In my store, shiny pennies are worth double."

"They are?" I asked, my spirits buoyed.

"Yep, shiny pennies are worth two."

And you know what? I believed him. I didn't just believe him because I was a kid and he was an adult. I believed him because of who he was. Words spoken by kind people have the ability to endure in our lives. It's over forty years later and when I see a shiny penny, I still instinctively think, *Shiny pennies are worth two.*

I know what you're thinking: shiny pennies aren't worth two, and the storekeeper was hatching a plot to ruin my grades in math class. But that's not the case. To him, shiny pennies were worth two, especially if they were my pennies. They might not be worth two at the next store. In his store, though, he made the rules, and he made that rule just for me.

Jesus was always talking about a reverse economy. He talked about how if you want to receive, you give. If you want to lead, you follow. That the poor are rich and you only really live for certain things if you are willing to die to them. What I learned from the storekeeper that day, in retrospect, is eerily familiar and shows me that we have more power than we think to make our own rules about life to live out the economy that Jesus put in place.

We each get to be the storekeeper, at least figuratively, and we decide who gets what and what things are worth. We get to decide that people, including ourselves, are worth more than others might figure and that following Jesus means doing the math differently sometimes. Because actually we're all on the same side of the counter when it comes to needing a little help and grace and a shiny penny now and then. We're the kid and we're the storekeeper.

....

CHAPTER 18

CATCHING A RIDE

I used to think life could be shared with anyone,
but now I know choosing the right people is pretty important.

Why does spellcheck make me capitalize satan's name? I don't want to. It's giving him too much credit.

I think satan exists, but I don't give him a lot of thought. Neither does the Bible, honestly. We talk about satan way more than the Bible ever talks about satan. I remember hearing some religious people scare little kids saying things like, "If you listen to heavy metal music, you're under satan's power." Or, "If you drink beer or smoke, then you're under satan's power." I'd never say that to a kid because, first of all, it would make them want to listen to heavy metal music, smoke, and drink. And second of all, it would make it harder for them to stop because they'd be convinced they were under satan's power.

When I think about satan, my thoughts go to how Jesus interacted with him in the desert. Jesus spoke with him for just a few seconds and then sent him away. Satan was a manipulator who wanted to control God, but Jesus had a relationship with God that satan didn't understand, and Jesus had no problem telling him off and getting rid of him. I think we should do the same.

That's all I have to say about satan. He gets too much airtime already.

••••◦◦◉◦◦••••

During college, I decided to take some time off and hitchhike around the country. It was a different time and back then lots of people were doing it. Lots of people were getting murdered too, which is why not so many people are doing it anymore.

One time, I decided to hitchhike from San Diego to the San Francisco Bay Area. I put my thumb out at San Diego State University, where I was going to college. I got several rides up the coast past Los Angeles and never had to wait for more than a few minutes between them. Mostly, people are nice and were willing to pull over. I had floppy ears and looked harmless enough too, which helped.

There's an unspoken rule when you hitchhike, more common sense, I guess. When a car pulls over to give you a ride, instead of telling the person driving where you need to go, you always ask the person where they're going. That will give you a second or two to check them out and see what they're like. If, for instance, they say they are going to the reptile convention or an assault rifle show, you can tell them you've been there already and catch a ride with somebody else.

At about Santa Barbara, I found myself stuck by the side of the highway for almost a day. After twenty-four hours, I was desperate to get moving again. Finally, a van pulled over to the shoulder toward my outstretched thumb. I wasn't thinking about anything except getting farther north, so I climbed in before the van had even come to a stop and threw my backpack in the space between the two front seats.

The guy driving looked about forty years old and had a huge beard. I was a little envious of his beard, actually, and imagined that someday I could have that kind of a wild man look. The windows weren't cracked, and it wasn't long before I caught wind of a toe-curling body odor. I did a quick pit check to make sure I wasn't the source. This guy could have knocked over a water buffalo at fifty yards. No matter. I was moving again and that was all I cared about.

As we picked up speed, I noticed the dashboard was covered in rose petals. *That's weird*, I thought. Was this guy a florist? I was guessing no; or business must have been slow because there were no other flowers inside the hollow, creepy, windowless van. On the driver's side, on top of a different stash of flower petals, was a picture of a guy's feet in a gold frame. If you're like me, you're probably thinking this is starting to get weird. *Why does someone have a picture of a dude's feet framed and set on top of flower petals?* I wondered. My best guess was that the bearded, stinky guy wasn't a podiatrist. My weirdometer needle was pegged.

After fiddling with my backpack a little and looking out the window, I asked the guy, "So where are you headed?" No answer.

This is precisely the reason I'd disciplined myself over the years to always ask someone where they're going before getting in with them. But on this occasion, I had been stuck in the ice plant by the highway long enough to go to seed and had somehow forgotten my rule. I let a few long moments pass in the off chance he was just taking his time to answer. After a while, I figured that the first question didn't land so I offered in a cheery voice, "So where are you coming from today? Isn't it a beauty? I love this time of year, don't you?" No answer again. Not a good sign.

I continued staring out the van window trying to put out an *I'm-not-freaked-out* vibe. Then, without any prompting, the driver turned his head really slowly like the bad guys do in horror movies.

"Do you really want to know who I am?" he said in a voice covered with emphysema and evil. "Sure," I bandied, trying to keep the mood light. We were going to be in the van for a while. Might as well get to know each other, find areas of common interest . . . you know . . .

"I'm satan."

"Oh," I said, kind of wishing I had some holy water in my canteen.

I know it wasn't the most probing response, but it was all I could come up with at the time. It also seemed more succinct than, "Stinks to be you. How's the plan to destroy the world coming together?" "How's your mom? Do you have a mom?"

In reality, I was totally freaked out. If I had packed my Depends I would have strapped them on. I told satan, who I was surprised to note was smaller than me, to pull over and let me out of his van. While it was nice to be moving again, I figured he wasn't ultimately headed where I wanted to go.

Satan acted like I hadn't said anything and kept on driving.

Playing it cool, I told satan more directly that I wanted him to pull over or I'd kick his butt. I think that it's good to be direct with satan, and I figured he probably had already heard all of the swear words I knew and maybe a few more. Satan pulled over, and I got out.

······◆······

Dust from his creepy, petal-filled, feet-idolizing van swirled around my face as he drove off. I took a shallow breath and tried to shake off the oddity of what I had just experienced. To be completely honest, I was thankful to be safe and I felt bad for whoever he was going to see next.

When I put my thumb out again, I was a little apprehensive. Eventually, a station wagon with peeling fake wood siding pulled over. It overshot me by a hundred yards and the reverse lights came on. The car rushed backward on the shoulder, crunching gravel the whole way.

The driver was a woman, and as I walked up to the window, I briefly scanned the back for pitchforks or any other evidence of the underworld. The only unusual thing was a really large black box behind the backseat. Suppressing the thought it might be the remains of a previous hitchhiker, I asked the woman where she was going, and she said she was on her way to a wedding in San Francisco. That sounded fairly safe, so I climbed in and we pulled onto the highway.

After a while, choosing to believe the best in my new traveling companion, I decided to get the conversation going. I asked in a casual voice that I'm sure sounded a little mousy, "Hey, what do you have in the back?" I was almost afraid of the answer before it came.

"It's my harp!" She beamed, turning toward me. "I'm doing the music for the wedding."

"Yeah?" I laughed. "Your harp. Of course."

I settled in my seat in her station wagon with fake wood siding, felt the warmth of the afternoon sun, grinned, and fell asleep.

••••◦━◉━◦••••

I learned something hitchhiking that day. I learned that even though I needed a ride to get somewhere, I had a lot of power over who I'd hitch a ride with. I know it sounds simple, but life is like that. You become like the people you hang around, and to a great degree, you end up going wherever they're headed. When there is someone else behind the steering wheel, it needs to be someone you'd trust with your life, because you've given a great deal of control over your life to them.

Psychologists are now theorizing about the separation of the brain and the mind. The brain is the stuff in your skull. But the mind, they say, works a lot like the Internet, a map of information collected from all of our experiences and interactions with other people. In other words, we become connected together and are influenced more than we think. If there's a dude who isn't great, I mean purely evil, it's important to get him out of your mind as fast as possible. Maybe that's why Jesus didn't give satan much airtime and just sent him packing instead.

All this is to say that we have a lot more power to decide who we do life with than some people think. And if you make a bad pick like I did, you need to do what it takes to get out of the car.

I don't mean to sound callous, because the bad ones need friends too. They just don't need you. Jesus doesn't give satan any grace. He just speaks the truth to him and then tells him to go away. If satan had come back saying he was sorry, that would be different; but of course he doesn't and he won't.

Some people learn to be altruistic and caring, and some people don't. You won't always know right away in the makeup of the people you meet. What I've decided is a pretty good idea is to just ask people where they're going before you get in with them. If they aren't heading where you want to end up, just wait in the ice plant by the highway a little while longer.

....

CHAPTER 19

JEEPOLOGY

I used to think the best teachers wore tweed jackets and smoked pipes, but now I know they flip over and leak.

One of my favorite teachers of all time wasn't a professor or a writer or even a religious leader. It was a car I owned. Specifically, it was a fire-engine-red Jeep jacked so high you could pull your groin getting in. It had a roll bar with a fire extinguisher strapped to it. This Jeep was all *guy*, a gear-and-metal manifesto of testosterone. If I could have installed seats made of beef jerky, I would have.

A year or two ago, as I was driving home from church, a car came darting out of a side street. It crashed into the side of my Jeep and caught me in front of the driver's side wheel. I didn't have any time to react. I couldn't swerve or reach for the fire extinguisher. I didn't even have time to call out to God. The Jeep started a barrel roll, and I went flying like someone was playing cornhole with my body. I'd like to say I had my seat belt on, but I didn't. (I know, Mom.) I was thrown out of the roof of the Jeep like a bullet from a rifle.

I regained my senses sitting upright on the asphalt, my arms propped up behind me like I was watching a ball game at the park on a summer day. The Jeep was upside down thirty feet away and the engine was racing like a phantom foot had the pedal to the floor. Oil and gas were everywhere. Because I'm a guy I had just one thought: *Blow up!* It's a guy thing, I suppose. Or maybe I really wanted to use the fire extinguisher. Alas, the Jeep didn't explode. Maybe next time.

Lots of other red vehicles started arriving. A fire truck, an ambulance, two kids on red bikes. I started feeling around to do another limb check. Everything being operational, I got up, dusted myself off, and walked toward the other car. The other driver was stunned and the window started slowly lowering.

Still clutching the steering wheel staring blankly forward was a small, frail woman. She was older, that was easy to see. I introduced myself. "Hi, I'm Bob. What's your name?" The stunned woman kept staring straight ahead, fists still clinched around the steering wheel.

"I-I'm Lynn . . . ," she stuttered.

"Lynn, are you okay?" I asked, leaning forward a little. Lynn was wafer thin. She couldn't have weighed a hundred pounds.

"I think I'm okay," she whispered. It wasn't surprising that this had left Lynn a little stunned. You see, Lynn was eighty-seven years old. She stood five-foot-nothing on her tiptoes and had been driving home from her seniors' exercise class. I tried to make eye contact with Lynn but didn't have success.

"I guess I forgot to stop," Lynn said, still clinching the steering wheel and staring forward. That was indeed correct. But who can be mad at someone like Lynn? Lynn turned her head toward me for the first time in our conversation and said with the seriousness of a grandmother and the surprise of a passerby, "Young man, do you know you went through the roof of your car?"

Oh yeah, right, that. I told her that's how I get out of my Jeep when I'm in a hurry. It saves me time by not having to open the door or swing my legs out. I'm a busy guy with things to do, you know . . .

I think Lynn expected me to scold her or tell her why she should have been more cautious, but instead, I put my hand on her shoulder. "Lynn," I said in a fitting voice, "I can't lie . . . That was *the coolest thing* that has *ever* happened to me!" She looked up and smiled for the first time. I tried to buoy her spirits by continuing, "If there was a ride at Disneyland like that, the line would be a mile long. Can we do it again next week? We'll meet right here in the intersection."

I asked again if she was okay and she said she was. The police were picking up pieces of my Jeep on a lawn across the street, behind a fence, and down a driveway a short distance away. One of the men from the fire truck helped us swap information. I was fine, so I figured I'd just walk home. Before I left, though, I called over to Lynn again, waved, and said not to worry. She was still shaken and seemed a little pensive. I walked back to her and asked what she was thinking.

"You know what I'm most concerned about?" she said, staring past me. "I don't think I'll ever be allowed to drive again."

I tried to empathize with her about what it would feel like and offered her some words of encouragement. Lynn continued, "You know what it is? I just don't want to be dependent on anyone."

I knew what she meant. I've never liked being dependent on anyone either. I could identify with what she was feeling. And then it dawned on me that I might be entering a season of dependence like Lynn was. The Jeep was totally thrashed as they rolled it right side up. Broken glass glittered on the street and chunks of metal were swept into piles as the Jeep was hauled to the junkyard. It would be weeks, or longer, before I'd have another set of wheels. Someone was going to have to tote me around now too. I said good-bye to Lynn as the tow truck, ambulance, and fire trucks pulled away, and walked home.

A few days later, I got a call on my cell phone. "Hello?" There was nothing at first, just empty silence. Then a brittle and remorseful voice crawled out of the phone.

"I am *so* sorry." It was Lynn.

"Lynn? Is that you? Hey, I'm fine. Really. Barely a bruise on me. I can't lie, the car could use a little paint, but really, don't give it another thought. You didn't need to call me. Honest." I tried to reassure her without much success and we hung up.

A few days later, I was taking a deposition and my phone rang again. It was the same silence followed by the frail, "I am *so* sorry."

"Lynn?" I asked. "Honest, it's all good. I'm fine. Really. You don't need to check on me. How are your grandkids? Really. No need to call." I was pleasant and said good-bye as we hung up, but I could tell this was going to keep happening. Lynn couldn't believe that I'd forgiven her and moved on.

I wondered what to do. I didn't want to change my cell phone number, but I also didn't want to get a call every other day from Lynn. So I hatched a plan. I had Lynn's address, so I called the local florist and had them put together a huge bouquet of flowers and deliver them to Lynn. I wrote a note and had it stuffed inside the flowers. I asked the delivery person to hang around long enough to report Lynn's reaction.

When Lynn came to the door, there was a huge basket of flowers waiting for her. She stood there more stunned than when she had flipped my Jeep. The basket of flowers was nearly bigger than she was, and when she opened the card she started to well up. The card said, "Dear Lynn, it was great running into you . . . Now stop calling me! Bob."

I think Lynn got the message. I was fine, and I wanted her to be fine too. I wanted her to forgive herself, to realize we all make mistakes. I'm glad I ran into Lynn, and I'm glad she kept calling too. It taught me something about faith. It taught me that when God is big enough and loves me enough to say He forgives me, I should actually believe Him. I mean, I shouldn't keep feeling bad about all of the times I've messed up because that's ignoring what God said, just like Lynn ignored what I said. When I don't trust God's forgiveness, it's kind of like saying I really don't believe He's that good. Lynn made me think I should stop asking God to forgive me over and over when He's made it clear He already has.

••••◦◆◦••••

Even though the Jeep was totaled, I bought it back from the insurance company for a couple thousand dollars and put some more red paint on it. It definitely had issues—it pulled to the left, for starters. I don't mean a little to the left. I mean, big-time left. If I needed to make a hard left turn into the driveway from the street, now all I had to do was hit the brakes. Second, wherever I parked the Jeep in the driveway, it would leave a puddle of oil behind. I'm no mechanic, but I get it. This car had been ridden hard and put away wet. It had been in a terrible collision. No wonder it leaked. There were other glitches, little things that only an owner would notice. Truth is, I wasn't really bothered by all this. The Jeep, despite its new handicaps, was *way* cooler, tougher, and more charming. And now it had a story. Before, it just looked like it had a story, but now it actually had one. And that story made it leaky.

I know it sounds goofy, but I want to be like that Jeep. I want to leak from having been hit by Jesus. From having something crazy happen to me, something that flipped my life upside down. I've met people like that, people who leak Jesus. Whenever you're around them, Jesus keeps coming up with words and with actions. I don't suppose everybody gets hit by Jesus, but those of us who have talk about Him differently. We start steering funny; we start leaking where we stand. And it's because we got thrown from our lives in a terrific collision.

••••◦•••••

I walked out of my house one Easter morning, like Mary to the tomb, and my Jeep was gone. It wasn't in the garage or in the driveway. None of the kids had taken the Jeep out for a spin and neither had Sweet Maria. I kept checking the driveway, which is only twenty feet long, thinking maybe I'd just overlooked it, or maybe it was down by the street. But it wasn't. It turns out it had been stolen the night before. I wasn't mad, just bummed.

Really bummed, because my Jeep and I had been through a lot together.

Standing in the driveway, I realized it was time to lean into dependence. I thought about Lynn and wondered how she was faring with her adjustment to the same. To be sure, I could have gone out and bought a car. I thought about replacing the Jeep the afternoon of the collision with Lynn, but something told me to stop. That same feeling welled up in me again as I gazed lovingly at the day-old oil stain in the driveway. Confession: I don't like needing anybody for anything, and I never have. I'm a lawyer with my own firm and am almost always on the giving side of an equation, rarely on the receiving side. And that's the way I like it. The morning after my Jeep was stolen, I decided, would be day one of learning a new lesson. I decided that I would learn about being dependent on others.

••••◆••••

It's been almost a year since my Jeep was stolen, and I didn't replace it. I wasn't trying to go green; I just wanted to learn about dependency. So I headed for the local skateboard shop. I got a Sector 9 longboard to get to work and back on. I didn't make it out of the driveway the first day before I fell. When I did, my first thought was that Lynn would come by and think it was her fault. But I'm getting pretty good now. Mind you, I can't grind the curbs, but I can do a wheelie. Except for skateboarding to work, for the next year I needed other people to help me get everywhere. Meetings, the airport, or even just to run a simple errand. If I wanted to go somewhere, I needed to borrow Sweet Maria's car or have one of the kids drop me off. This let Maria know even more deeply that she's needed, and it made us work together on just about everything. I had to borrow somebody else's stuff to do just about anything. For a guy who likes not needing anything, that's pretty humbling. Even my own kids told me to put gas in their cars when I asked to borrow them—"and, Dad, don't flip it." That's what they'd say with a wink as they tossed me the keys.

Being dependent has helped me see the world in a whole new way. I'm not as rushed as I used to be. I usually leave for work and return with a big grin because I'm the only middle-aged lawyer on the block carrying a laptop and riding a skateboard to and from work, carving turns along the way.

····◆·····

I still miss the Jeep. Sometimes, when the phone rings, I secretly hope it's the police and they're calling to say they've found it. There's an equally good chance, though, that it's just Lynn on the phone again saying she's sorry.

I doubt I'll ever see my Jeep again, but it doesn't matter; the lessons it taught me are living on in its absence. I'm better now at receiving forgiveness, I hopefully leak Jesus a little bit more, and I'm certainly closer to my family. To be honest, though, I should probably get a car pretty soon. At my house everybody scatters when I walk into the kitchen, grabbing their keys, shoving toast into their mouths, and running out the door or to their rooms. No matter. If I can't get a lift from someone at my house, I'll just call Lynn and see if I can borrow her car.

....

CHAPTER 20

TEN-YEAR-OLD ADVENTURES

I used to think knowing God was like going on a business trip with Him,
but now I know He's inviting me on an adventure instead.

Sweet Maria and I made a pact early in our marriage: when each of our children reached ten years old, they got to go on a trip with dad. We called it a "ten-year-old adventure." The idea was simple. The kids got to pick something in the world that captured their imaginations, fanned their whimsy, or sparked their curiosity, and then we'd just go do it together. There was no planning, no preparation, no thinking about all the details. We'd just go do it.

Lindsey was the first to turn ten and loved to have tea parties at the house. She'd heard of an event called "high tea" that some fancy hotels put on where you dress up and eat finger sandwiches and drink tea. She asked me if I would take her.

"You bet. Where do you want to go?"

"I'm not sure. Where do people drink lots of tea?" Lindsey asked.

"London, I think" was my best guess.

"Great, that's what I pick for my ten-year-old adventure. When do we leave?"

I got on the phone and found a couple cheap tickets on British Airlines to London. A week later, we were off. Most great adventures work that way. You don't plan them, you don't wait to get all the details right, you just do them.

On a ten-year-old adventure, the goal is to do everything that you can in the time you've got. You don't know where you'll stay or what you'll eat and all the other details that usually accompany a trip. For three days, the kids and I commit to learn about each other and the world through what we experience in it, not what we've read about it or planned into it. There aren't any other rules. That's what makes it an adventure, not a program.

There's a special relationship between a dad and a daughter, something God designed on purpose, I think. It's not lost on me that of all of the names God could have asked us to call Him, we most often refer to Him as "Father." I think that's because He has the same kind of relationship in mind for us that I had in mind for my kids. I think a father's job, when it's done best, is to get down on both knees, lean over his children's lives, and whisper, "Where do you want to go?"

Every day God invites us on the same kind of adventure. It's not a trip where He sends us a rigid itinerary, He simply invites us. God asks what it is He's made us to love, what it is that captures our attention, what feeds that deep indescribable need of our souls to experience the richness of the world He made. And then, leaning over us, He whispers, "Let's go do *that* together."

Lindsey and I landed in London and hit the ground running— there was no waiting to counteract the jetlag and there wasn't any luggage to get. We saw everything we could possibly cram in to three days. We went to Buckingham Palace, the River Thames, the Tower of London, the huge London Eye Ferris wheel. We ran through Hyde Park barefoot, we tried to make a guard in a bearskin hat giggle, we took in a play in the West End, we ate fish and chips, and we said "quite" as we toasted each other with soda pops lifting our pinky fingers toward the Queen. We didn't rest, we didn't sleep, and we didn't know where we'd stay, but none of that mattered. And of course, the last thing we did before heading back to the airport was have high tea at the Ritz.

We sat bleary eyed at a small, beautifully apportioned, perfectly British table. A stoic server brought us our goodies, and I only made it through one finger sandwich before I looked across the table and saw a ten-year-old girl who would be thirty-five some day taking her own kids on the same kind of adventures. And I thought about what God must see when He looks at us. Like I saw my ten-year-old turning thirty-five, I imagine He sees who we'll all become, too, if we start RSVPing yes to His invitations and go after those things He's made us to love. It's not all planned out for us either, and that's where most people get too nervous to take the next step. But know this: when Jesus invites us on an adventure, He shapes who we become with what happens along the way.

Richard turned ten, and he had barely blown out his birthday candles before he turned to me with the steely resolve of a guy who had just climbed Everest and said two simple words: "Half Dome."

Rich wanted to hike up the back side of Half Dome for his ten-year-old adventure. He didn't want to go at any old time either—he wanted to do it in the middle of the winter in a snow storm. I liked his grit. We went to an outfitter that afternoon and picked out a backpack, a tent, a couple sleeping bags, and some boots. That night we turned off the sprinklers and set up base camp in our backyard, cooked freeze-dried peaches over our camping stove, told manly stories, and figured out our route up Half Dome from a topographical map neither of us knew how to read. The same rules were in play for his ten-year-old adventure. There would be no stopping, no sleeping, no details. Just a big idea, a willingness to go, and a father who wanted to take him there.

We kept our eyes on the weather. One evening when it looked like the first big storm of the season was going to clobber Yosemite, we frantically packed the car, hopped in, and drove all night. We had all of the necessary food groups with us—candy bars and In and Out Burgers—and spent our time on the drive talking about what it would be like to summit Half Dome in the snow together.

We pulled up to the foot of Half Dome just as dawn was breaking over Yosemite valley. Within minutes we had our back-packs on and started hiking. By the late afternoon, the storm we had predicted moved in on us. As the storm settled in, we made camp at the base of a steep section of the granite monolith and decided we'd hunker down for the night and make a push to the top in the morning. That night, we slept in spurts as more than one bear circled the tent looking for any food not properly hung in the trees. Thankfully they weren't interested in human-stuffed sleeping bag burritos. The bears would occasionally brush up against the nylon tent, but we both pretended that it wasn't a big deal to us (even though it really was). That's what guys who are together on an adventure do—they don't make a big deal out of everything. The big deal is that they're together.

Rich and I woke in the morning to a thick blanket of snow. After a brew of coffee for me and a couple chocolate bars for Rich, we headed farther up the mountain above the tree line. What gives Half Dome its name is that it looks like a huge marble-shaped circle cut in half from top to bottom. It's the reason climbing it can be treacherous, too, because there are no trees and no footholds anywhere on the marble. The layer of overnight ice and snow made climbing even sportier.

On the way up, Rich was tethered to me by a bright red climbing rope. I would climb a few steps, kicking footholds into the snow, and then Rich would climb in my steps and kick some of his own as we made our way up the steep slope. When we got to our high point, we could see an even bigger storm bearing down on us and knew we'd soon be in whiteout conditions.

On our way down, I would take a couple steps and then Rich would take a couple steps. Each time I would take Rich's small feet with my hands and guide them from below into the next step we'd kicked together into the snow. We were too excited to be afraid and too engaged in the moment to be thinking of anything else. We made it to the valley eight hours later and drove home only stopping for some more In and Out Burgers.

I think God is more of a Half Dome traveler than a Hampton

Inn traveler. Jesus doesn't invite us on a business trip. Instead, He says let's go after those things that inspire and challenge you and let's experience them together. You don't need a lot of details or luggage or equipment, just a willingness to go into a storm with a Father who's kicking footholds into the steep sides of our problems while we kick a couple in ourselves too. He guides us into those footholds with His strong hands while we're safely tethered to Him by a bright red rope of grace, which holds us securely. Somehow in all of this, the terrain we navigate doesn't seem as scary either, because when we're on an adventure with God we're too excited to be afraid and too engaged to be thinking of anything else.

••••◉••••

Adam turned ten and I heard him say he wanted to ride a motorcycle in the desert. That sounded simple enough, a little tame for Adam, actually. Apparently, though, I had heard wrong. He said he wanted to ride motorcycles *across* the desert—a big difference. I tried to block out the pictures that came to mind of sun-bleached bones, cow skulls, and guys clawing across the sand with empty canteens and tattered shirts wrapped around their heads. Honestly, I wasn't sure if it could be done, but I figured we'd find out soon enough. We gassed up the motorcycles and left the next day.

Any activity where you could lose an eye or a limb is Adam's love language. So when we got to the desert, we headed for the sand dunes. These dunes were different from the ten-footers I rolled down at the beach when I was a kid. These were seven hundred feet tall. Once you start up one of these monsters in a motorcycle, you need to get to the top without stopping. If you hesitate or try to pause halfway, the result is that you, with the motorcycle on top of you, cartwheel all the way down to the bottom. It's a pass/fail course because there's no in between.

After topping several huge sand dunes with Adam and then losing track of him for a moment, I heard his motor racing just over the next dune. I made my way over to where the noise was coming from and it was apparent in an instant that Adam was planning to jump from the top of one sand dune to the top of another. I was yelling "No!" across a canyon of sand, and it felt like a movie-style slow motion sequence kicked in as Adam raced through the gears and hit the peak of the dune doing more than 60 miles per hour. Almost immediately, Adam and his machine separated. It was quite a sight, really. He had the look of both Superman and a gut-shot pheasant at the same time. Adam landed 120 feet later surrounded by the scrap metal remains of what he was riding. His first words when I rushed over to him were "That was awesome." And you know what? *It was.* Even though things didn't go as planned and Adam crashed and burned, there was a huge sense of accomplishment for him in that.

····◆····

I think God sees our failed launches in the same way. He sees us flying over the handlebars in slow motion, and while He never wants to see us hurt, He knows it can happen from time to time when we live a life of total engagement. I think He sees the outcomes before they happen too and calls to us over the noise in our lives warning of something that won't go well. Like Adam, we often don't hear the warning call and race through the gears only to find ourselves upside down in the sand. After we come to, He dusts us off, helps us to our feet, and He hears us say, "That was awesome." More than once when I've crashed and burned, I've felt Him lean in closely to me after picking up the pieces of my life and whisper back to me, "You know what? *It was.*"

•••••●●●•••••

The kids and I learned about young boys and girls in India who were on a different type of ten-year-old adventure—the worst kind, really. Slave traders in India, called Mudelalis, make slaves of young children my kids' ages. In order to work off an illegal, so-called "debt" of as little as ten dollars, peasant families would often give a son or daughter to a slave trader as a bonded laborer. Trafficking of this type is illegal in India, but tens if not hundreds of thousands of low cast children are caught up in it each year. From the work I was doing in the country, I learned of four children being held in a cave behind the house of a slave trader named Gopal. The kids and I left for India that week to try to get them out.

We traveled to Chenai in Southern India and from there to a small nondescript village fifteen hours into the bush. A local contact agreed to sneak these children out of the cave at one in the morning when the slave trader wouldn't notice they were gone. We arrived at the meeting spot, and I watched out the windows as my kids fingerprinted the children and documented their stories so that their wrongful imprisonment could be reported to the local head of government.

Two weeks later, we received photographs of soldiers raiding Gopal's filthy cave to free the four children. The soldiers also freed thirty others in the local village who were under the control of other slave traders. That's the way love is—not unlike loaves and fishes, its impact multiplies.

Even though Jesus' disciples were older, they must have felt like my kids did on their ten-year-old adventures. They saw joy and suffering, triumph and tragedy, and in the end there was just a man, an idea, and an invitation without a lot of details. The disciples were unschooled and ordinary like my kids, like all of us. Yet they didn't need all the details because they were on an adventure with a father who wanted to take them. You don't need to know everything when you're with someone you trust.

That's probably why Jesus' disciples never said they were on a missions trip. I think they knew love already had a name and they didn't need a program or anything else to define it. We don't either. The kind of adventure Jesus has invited us on doesn't require an application or prerequisites. It's just about deciding to take up the offer made by a father who wants us to come.

....

CHAPTER 21

HEARING AID

I used to think God wouldn't talk to me,
but now I know I'm just selective with what I choose to hear.

During my first year of marriage, Sweet Maria was convinced I had a hearing problem, so we made an appointment to have my hearing tested. A week later, I showed up at the hearing doctor's office and was ushered into a very official-looking testing studio. They gave me some high-tech headphones and a handset with a red button on the top to press when I heard a tone.

The doctor didn't know how bad my hearing was, and just as a joke, I was going to make her sign to me where to sit or keep pointing to my ears and shaking my head like I couldn't hear her. I decided against it at the last minute—next time I'm going to.

After the doctor put the headphones on me, she went back to her station and watched me through a glass window. I was hoping she would spin up some Van Halen, but she sent me very boring sounds through the headphones to determine which ones were within my audibility range.

We rang though tone after tone. Chalkboard-scratching horrible sounds. Shrill, dog whistle pitches that made me want to howl. Low tones Barry White would've envied. I was doing fine on the test to begin with, but as we went along I found a way to cheat. Each time the doctor sent a tone though the system, she would look up to see if I heard it. I pressed the button every time she looked up. But it didn't matter, I could hear the tones anyway. I was acing this thing. I was sure that if there were audibility Olympics, I'd be the torchbearer leading us all into the stadium.

After a lengthy test covering every frequency range known to man, we sat down together to go through the results. The doctor confirmed that I indeed could hear perfectly. It turned out that my "hearing problem" was nothing of the sort. I could hear well. I was just being lazy and selective in what I heard, tuning out anything I didn't want to hear. During the diagnostic report, Sweet Maria was tapping her foot and giving me the eye. She told the doctor she had been telling me for some time that my hearing was just fine; I just wasn't listening. I don't remember hearing her say that.

I realized that what was understandably so frustrating for Sweet Maria was a similar issue I have with God. What I mean is, I only hear the things from God I want to hear, and it makes me wonder if He doesn't think I'm going a little bit deaf.

God doesn't speak to me with a voice to make audio needles move, but there are times when I've sensed something down deep, almost like a tuning fork has just been pinged in my soul.

It's not just one of those "I know because I know" things either. I think we can triangulate on the unmistakable tugs of God's voice because we know other things about His character and nature. For instance, we know God loves us and how right forgiveness feels. We also know some truths about the world, like the love we have in our family and how we've always liked rainy days and cheeseburgers, that sort of stuff. From there, we can get a sense of how God has wired us and use a combination of our hearts and His truths to move ourselves in a certain direction.

Some people describe their relationship with God as an ongoing narrative that includes an audible discussion. I lived with a bunch of surfers during college in Southern California and they would describe hearing God's voice. It often went something like this . . . "So I said, 'Hey, God, what's up with this?' And then God said, 'Hey, dude, don't worry about it; it'll be cool.'" (God apparently addressed surfers as "dude" or "hey man.") And then they'd say back to God, "No way!?" And then God said back to them, "Yahweh" or something equally biblical.

All of this head-faked me for a while, to be honest, because when I listened for God's voice I didn't hear anything. No cosmic whispers. No movie reels with subtitles. No still, small voice, no booming voice, and no one addressing me as "dude" or "hey man" either. I wondered if these surfers were cheating the same way I did in the doctor's office. Maybe they were pretending to hear just because someone like me was looking.

It's not that I haven't asked God to talk to me. I've asked for a paragraph, a sentence, a phrase, a word. I've even asked if I could just buy a vowel. I've told God that I wouldn't tell anyone if He would just say one audible thing to me. We'd keep it all attorney-client privileged . . . yet still, I haven't heard a thing.

So rather than spending time wondering why I don't hear audible voices, I just try to listen harder with my heart, and I've realized a couple of things that seem kind of obvious now. God doesn't talk to me in an audible voice because God isn't a human being; He's God. That makes sense to me, because human beings are limited and God isn't limited at all. He can communicate to us in any way He wants to anytime He wants to. Through flowers, other people, an uncomfortable sense, a feeling of joy, goose bumps, a newfound talent, or an appreciation we acquire over time. It doesn't need to be a big mystical thing like my surfer buddies made it out to be.

I haven't seen a combination of tree limbs that looked like John the Baptist or a cloud formation resembling Jesus. Honestly, they just look like branches and clouds to me. But I do see the beauty in them and the beauty that's everywhere, that God made for me and you. I especially see evidence of God in other people's lives. What's beautiful about them always looks an awful lot like God to me. I wonder if the people listening for voices or looking for cloud shapes miss the whisper of God's creation, somehow thinking it's a lesser form of communication, like a text message rather than a whole book on tape. It could just be me, but in all of this and despite what feels like a handicap at times, I can almost read His lips inaudibly saying to me, *"I love you this much."*

The more I've listened to God, the more I've realized I don't always catch what God is up to in real time either. Some people speak with a great deal of authority about what God is doing *right now*. I'm always amazed because I can never figure out God that quickly. I usually understand what God is doing by seeing it through the rearview mirror. Only then can I connect the dots, and even then, it's a pretty dodgy sketch. Maybe that's why the

Bible described what we are often doing as looking through a mirror dimly. The Bible says that right now we only know "in part" and that one day, after we've gone, we'll know "in full." That makes more sense to me because it means our understanding will always have gaps and gaps are good because they leave room for God to fill in the spaces.

But until all those gaps are filled in, I need to operate on my best guess. I need to listen to that internal tuning fork. Some folks might cringe to think that much of what we do is a best guess about God's desires or aims. But I'm just being honest. Why fake it? I take the fixed points of His character and my particular hardwiring and extrapolate from there. There are plenty of fixed points too, so we don't need to get worried. There are letters written from prison cells and gospel accounts about how God sees the world and sees us. There are accounts of what Jesus said and sometimes what He didn't say. All of these are good signposts, and they should be enough. Besides, we shouldn't speak with an assurance we don't really have like we're God's PR agent and risk misquoting the God of the universe, who could turn us into a pile of salt. This all helps me be a little more respectful and humble when I'm attributing something to God.

Most of the characters in Scripture didn't hear from God in an audible voice. Even though at one point Moses got the audio version of God and a stone tablet. What the Bible describes about Moses' encounter with God is much like what God regularly does to me. That is, God didn't give Moses what he asked for. Moses wanted to see God's face just like I want to hear His voice. In response, God told Moses to get in a big crack in a rock and God passed by. But when He did, He covered Moses' eyes with His hand so that all Moses got to see was God's back. I feel the same way.

I think God passes by me a lot, and it serves to show me the direction He's going. We don't always know where He's headed or what to expect along the way. But I think *direction* is the point, the part, and whole of it. He wants followers, not just onlookers or people taking notes. Plus, I think God knows that if I found out more than just the direction He was going, I'd probably try to beat Him there. And if He spoke to me with something audible, I'd probably mess it up and mishear Him.

I was with my daughter, Lindsey, at the airport recently. We were talking about whether or not God had a plan for our lives like lots of people talk about. So I sent a text message to one of Lindsey's friends. "Hi, I'm sitting here with Lindsey" the text message started. (I didn't want to creep her out.) "I want to know what your plan for my life is." A few minutes later, I got a text back from her friend. It just said "????" I could picture her friend thinking, *My plan for Bob's life? Why would I have one?*

Lindsey and I kept talking for a few minutes and I got another text message from her friend. It said, "Bob, my plan for your life is that you would love God." Then a few minutes later, I got another one: "Bob, my plan for your life is that the things you are doing in Uganda would go just great"; and a few minutes later, still another: "My plan for your life is that you would love your family." Each of the text messages simply took something this friend knew about me, things she knew about God, things she knew I loved and were good for me, and she simply rolled them into a plan, or stated differently, a hope and a direction for me.

It was as though she was saying, "Bob, you know those things that have pinged you? Those gifts that are beautiful? Those countries and people who are most important to you? The God you love? Keep moving toward those." And what she was pointing me toward wasn't mystical or elusive. She just kept pointing me back toward the God I'm trying to follow, the people and the places I've been drawn to, and the hopes that have emerged within me. That's what Jesus does too; He points us toward Himself.

I don't think God is giving me the silent treatment because He's mad. I think God's hope and plan for us is pretty simple to figure out. For those who resonate with formulas, here it is: add your whole life, your loves, your passions, and your interests together with what God said He wants us to be about, and that's your answer. If you want to know the answer to the bigger question—what's God's plan for the whole world?—buckle up: it's us.

We're God's plan, and we always have been. We aren't just supposed to be observers, listeners, or have a bunch of opinions. We're not here to let everyone know what we agree and don't agree with, because, frankly, who cares? Tell me about the God you love; tell me about what He has inspired uniquely in you; tell me about what you're going to do about it, and a plan for your life will be pretty easy to figure out from there. I guess what I'm saying is that most of us don't get an audible plan for our lives. It's way better than that. We get to be God's plan for the whole world by pointing people toward Him.

Because I don't get the audible version of God, I also look for evidence of where Jesus has been. It's similar to what Luke told a young guy named Theophilus in the Bible. Luke told his young friend to look for many convincing proofs that Jesus is still alive. As a lawyer that sounds a lot like collecting evidence, dusting for divine fingerprints. So I've been dusting for fingerprints of Jesus ever since. I look for them in the things I think I understand as well as the things I know I don't understand at all. I'm trying to figure out the direction an inaudible God is moving in, and I'm using every shard of evidence He's left in the Bible, in my life, and all around me to do it. And you know what? It works.

I have an alarm clock that talks to me, I have a computer that talks to me, and I have books on tape that talk to me. I even had a navigation system in my car before it got stolen that talked to me. I could pick the accent. I like the one that sounds like my British butler is steering the car. Just for fun, when I had guests in the car, I'd sometimes switch the language to have it talk to me in Mandarin Chinese. And you know what? We still got to where we were headed. Like my communication with God, I don't need to hear words I recognize all the time to know what direction God wants me to go, because there's all kinds of other information I can triangulate off of.

Could God speak to me audibly if He wanted to? You bet, and I hope He does sometime; I'll let you know. Probably in a book called *God Talked to Me*. Until then, it seems that what God does most of the time when He has something to say is this . . . He doesn't pass us messages, instead He passes us each other.

....

CHAPTER 22

THE PUPPETEER

I used to be afraid that if I was authentic I might take a hit,
but now I know that being real means I will take a hit.

W hen the kids were growing up, I used to pass by this fancy
art gallery pretty often. I'd always glance in and admire
the handiwork of some talented people. One day, as I
walked past, I saw the most magnificent painting I'd ever seen
before hanging on the wall. It was called *The Puppeteer*. I'm no
art collector, that's for sure, but it looked like a pretty cool painting to me. I squished my nose against the window each time I
passed by the gallery and mouthed the words against the glass:
"Yes, you will be mine."

The Puppeteer is an oil painting of an old guy with his family gathered around, and he's dangling a marionette from strings, making everybody laugh. He looks like he's telling everybody a great story. I liked the painting because I've always imagined myself kind of like the puppeteer with my kids and their children gathered around someday. The painting also reminds me of how Jesus invites us to gather around Him as He tells captivating stories about a better life, a bigger life, and a greater love.

I asked the guy at the gallery how much the painting was. He started giving me his sales pitch in a muddled accent, and it was hard to follow what he was saying. He told me that it's not called a painting but a "piece." I guess they change the name when something is that expensive. Whatever.

According to him, the guy who created the painting was an eighty-year-old master painter from Europe. I had looked him up and knew that much was true. The sales guy also said the artist was going blind (yeah, sure). He was laying it on pretty thick and said something about the artist painting this piece with a special paintbrush. I was waiting for him to say the paintbrush was made of a single hair from the tail of a unicorn. I get it. It's a really nice painting, which at least explains why it cost more than my first four cars. Still, I wanted that painting more than I wanted food. So I started saving.

It took about a year to save the money. For the final bit, I was ready to put our family dog on eBay, but after a family meeting, that idea was shut down. No matter. I finally called the guy at the gallery and told him I'd be coming by to pick up the painting that afternoon. When I walked into the gallery there were two paintings waiting for me, two exact paintings of *The Puppeteer*. I didn't understand. "Why are there two paintings?" I asked the guy with the muddled accent.

"Well," he said, managing with absolute ease to sound conde-scending and slick, "ze one on the left is ze real one. It's museum qualeetay. It's very expensive, almost priceless. You don't want to hang ze original where it might get damaged, so you put ze original in a vault. Zis other one, however," he said as he slapped the identical painting irreverently, "iz ze fake one and iz ze one you put up on the wall for everyone to see."

"I get a fake one along with the original?" I asked. I had never even heard of such a thing.

"Yez," he shot back.

Well, let me ask you, dear reader: which of the two paintings would you put up on the wall? Me too. I hung the real one and threw the fake one in a closet somewhere.

I get why the guy at the gallery wanted me to hang the fake one and hide the real one to keep it safe. If the original was put out and damaged, it would be a huge loss. This was original art from a master artist who was not long for this earth. It was rare, one of a kind, and irreplaceable.

·••●•••••

If you come over to the Goff house, come armed. We have incredible rubber-band wars. Not the paper route, elementary school kind of rubber-band wars. We go nuclear and no one is safe. When the kids stretch a rubber band a foot or so, it can raise a welt the size of a strawberry wherever you get hit.

I start every morning sitting in a certain chair at my house. It's opposite from where I hung the original Puppeteer painting. I love starting each day with a cup of coffee, a small fire, and see-ing my friend, the Puppeteer, delighting his family. Through the divided light windows, I watch the sun come up over the water with colors sometimes too beautiful to be real. Two windows perfectly frame the Puppeteer painting that invites onlookers to see what appears to be his next show, which has just started.

When I look at the Puppeteer, it reminds me of what the future looks like for me. It reminds me of what's valuable in life. It reminds me of stories like the kind Jesus told. And I think about how much I love that it's the original hanging on the wall, not the fake one.

I woke up one morning awhile ago, poured my coffee, lit a small fire, and took in the beauty of the predawn colors draping over the bay as I took to my usual morning spot. As I lifted my eyes toward the Puppeteer, ready to wish a good morning to my friend, my jaw dropped.

The night before, as best I could tell, the Puppeteer had taken a rubber band right in the face. I'm not kidding. There was a mark right in the middle of his almost priceless forehead.

I gasped and spilled coffee on myself as I sprung from my chair to get a closer look. Indeed, the Puppeteer had taken a head shot. To his credit, the Puppeteer didn't drop the puppet even though mortally wounded. Now, my kids say they didn't do it and think it was my rubber band that took him out. But I've sent the painting off to the FBI crime lab—it was the kids. At least that's my story.

It's been awhile since the Puppeteer took a hit, but I still enjoy my morning routine. I still sit in my favorite chair every morning, have a coffee, light my fire, watch the sun rise, and look at my favorite piece of art, the original Puppeteer painting. I'm still taken by its beauty. But do you think I see the damage when I look at the Puppeteer each morning? Not at all. I'm not mad or disappointed in the least. The reason is simple: the rubber-band mark reminds me exactly and fondly of my kids.

I see my kids and the engaged life we've spent together so far. I see all the mischief, the whimsy, and the spontaneous combustion that is their hallmark. I see the kids lying in wait for me, rubber bands pulled tight at the top of the stairs and around the corners when I come home after work at night. Truth be known, I like the original Puppeteer painting now more with the rubber-band mark on it.

There have been times in my life when I've tried to do good and it hasn't worked out the way I thought it would. I've gotten into a lot of mischief and taken chances and have even taken some big risks. In the process, sometimes I've let people down or things I've done didn't go well and I've taken a rubber band or two to the head. We all have. But after the Puppeteer painting got shot, I realized that God doesn't think any less of us when things don't go right. Actually, I think He plans on it. What He doesn't plan on is us putting a fake version of ourselves out there to take the hit. God is the master artist and made an original version of us, a priceless one that cost everything to create. A version that can't and won't be created again.

He asks us to hang that version of ourselves for everyone to see. Despite our inherent beauty, each of us is tempted to hide the original so we won't get damaged. I understand why, I really do. And the fake version of us, it's not worthless. It's just *worth less* because it's only a copy of the real us, a version we don't care about as much. When we hang the fake version out there, it's not the version God created. In that sense, it's like an imposter, a poser, a stunt double is standing in for us and telling the world that this is the best we've got, or the best we'll risk. And when we put the cheap, fake version of ourselves out there, most of the time it probably comes off to God like a bad Elvis impersonation.

The Bible says people who are friends of God are new creations. The way I heard it's supposed to work is that old version of us goes away and a new original is painted. I can understand that picture better now, because I've purchased an expensive painting, and I've also had a cheap copy thrown in so I could hide the real one. What I know now is that our infinite value, the original masterwork that we are, is placed in us because God is the master artist, not us. The best we could muster ourselves would be a fake.

God invites us to be new creations, original art, and to live a life of engagement. He says to leave the cheap imitation in a closet somewhere. He doesn't say when you hang the real you out there—the priceless one—that things will go great either. It's pretty clear from watching Jesus' followers past and present that when you risk the real you, you'll probably take a hit. God did when He hung Jesus out there. But one thing I do know is this: when we do take hits, and we will, God isn't going to think less of us. Instead, He gets up early, lights a fire, sits in His favorite chair, and gazes at the original masterpiece He made in us. And you know what? He loves us even more, rubber-band marks and all.

....

CHAPTER 23

FRIENDS, WELCOME HOME

I used to think following God required a lot of navigation,
but now I know all I need is a line and a circle.

Ever since high school I wanted to go on a really long sailing trip. In fact, a buddy and I decided one day we'd sail across the Pacific Ocean to Hawaii. Since 1906, every other year, there's been a race from Los Angeles to Hawaii. It's called the Transpac Race. For safety reasons, the rules require that competing boats be forty-five feet or longer with a full crew. But on this particular year, they changed the rules to allow smaller boats to go, so we signed up to enter the race in a thirty-five-foot sailboat.

Now, thirty-five feet doesn't sound that small at first, until you figure out that it's about twice the length of a Toyota Camry and a little narrower. After you subtract the pointy end, it's about the size of a 1960s VW bus filled with twenty-five huge bags of sails, a life raft, six cases of Stagg chili, six hundred bottles of water, five guys, and a porta-potty. Come to think of it, that's what a lot of 1960s VW buses still look like inside.

The plan was simple. We'd sail twenty-six hundred miles across the ocean in our VW bus at seven miles an hour while God threw three garbage cans full of ice-cold water in the windows every couple of minutes; and while all this happened, we'd just eat chili and tell manly stories about ourselves.

There were supposed to be six guys on the trip. None of us knew how to navigate and we didn't want to miss Honolulu, so we asked a friend who was a navigator on a US Navy destroyer to come with us. He said yes, so we had our ringer. We were styling.

Navigating the race was no small task. You can't just use a GPS to figure out where you are. Instead, there's a requirement that each of the boats steer by the stars and the sun. To do this, our navigator had a couple feet of books, mostly almanacs estimating where the sun or planets would be at any particular time. From these and with the help of a sextant, which locates where you are in relation to the sun and stars, you could do some complicated math and figure out exactly where you were. Unfortunately, a few days before the race, the navy changed our navigator's orders. He couldn't come. We were no longer styling.

The race was going to start soon, so that next day we drew straws to see who would replace the navigator. I've hated straws ever since. With our navy navigator leaving, he took all his gear with him too. The stacks of books, the knowledge, and even his fancy sextant. He let me hold the sextant once, and I remember pointing it toward the sky like Galileo, but I had no clue how to

use it. We really were in trouble, so I ran to the local marine supply store and for fifteen dollars bought a plastic sextant and got
twenty minutes of instruction from the guy in aisle three on how
to use it. How tough could it be, after all?

He said that there's a complicated way to use a sextant properly. It involves looking to the heavens and finding a few fixed
points. Then you look up what you found in the couple of feet of
books and do lots of math. If you do all of the calculations right,
you can figure out pretty close to where you are, which is amazing, actually. Then there are a hundred nuances to be factored in
from there to figure out precisely where you are: what time of year
it is, what ocean and hemisphere you are in, the wave height at the
time you take the sighting, how far above the surface of the water
you are standing, what you had for lunch, and your favorite color,
I suppose. My head was going foggy as the guy on aisle three ran
through a list of the things I would need to consider to make an
accurate computation of our exact location. I wondered what this
guy was doing selling boat parts, anchors, and bottom paint. He
was talking like a guy who had a doctorate in astrophysics.

After twenty minutes, I interrupted Copernicus and explained
that we were leaving for Hawaii in three days, and I didn't follow
much of what he'd just said about how to calculate my location.
"Isn't there a faster way to use the sextant to get a trustworthy
guesstimate?" I asked. "Like Columbus or the Vikings or Kon
Tiki did? I'm sure they didn't get wrapped around the axle with
all of the details or have two feet of books to look at to figure out
where they were. Did they even have books then?"

The guy in aisle three leaned forward and hushed his voice
as if he were inviting me into the witness protection program.
"Okay, here's what you do . . ." He said I should take the plastic

sextant up on the deck, point it toward the sky, and take a reading at five minutes to noon, at noon, and at five minutes after noon. By doing this, I'd have a couple of fixed points from the sun and from there I could figure out where we were within a circle of give or take sixty miles.

Water covers about 140 million square miles of the entire surface of earth. So I figured if I could find myself inside a sixty-mile circle somewhere along a line pointing toward Hawaii that sounded close enough. My overall plan was to head west until we made landfall; it seemed simple and straightforward enough. There are lots of Hawaiian islands, so I figured, honestly, if we got to any of them instead of making our first landfall in Japan, it would be a win.

The other thing I got at the marine store before I left for Hawaii was a map. It was as big as a table, but it didn't really have much information on it. It just had a huge empty space between the West Coast on one side and Hawaii on the other side. I'm no oceanographer, but I figured that everything in between was water. There was a compass rose printed in the upper corner. It had a big *N* at the top, so I deduced it was telling me which way was north—good to know. Of course, when all you have is water around you, there are no landmarks to help you orient your direction. I'm not sure how much an *N* would help us get to Hawaii.

No matter, I guess. I got a yardstick and put one end on the starting line in Los Angeles and the other end I put on Diamond Head in Oahu. Then I drew a straight line. That was easy enough. From the compass rose, I figured out what heading to steer, and with that, I took my map, my ruler, my plastic sextant, and headed for the boat.

There's a navigation technique that helped me on the Transpac Race and has also pointed me generally in the right direction in life. The concept in sailing is known as "dead reckoning." The idea is a simple one, so it's right in my wheelhouse. It involves using your compass to take a bearing off a couple of fixed points and then drawing a line from each one to you in order to determine where you are.

When I don't know the answer to where I am or what God wants me to be doing, which is often, I try to get a bearing on at least a couple of fixed points that I can trust. One is Jesus. I know it sounds like a canned Sunday school answer, and I tend not to like those, but it's true. I take a bearing off what I know about Jesus. But it's a Jesus who isn't encumbered by religion, denomination, and cultural overlays. I look at what He had to say about where I am and then I draw a line from Jesus to me.

The other fixed point I use is a group of people I feel God has dropped into my life, kind of like a cabinet. These people have their particular areas of wisdom and experience, and I use them to bounce ideas off of and get their input. In turn, I'm on the cabinets of many of my friends and family members too. For instance, I'm on my daughter Lindsey's cabinet. I've appointed myself to be in charge of homeland security for her. The people on my cabinet help me do some dead reckoning in my life because I take a bearing on their counsel as another fixed point in my life and draw a line from them to me.

From these points, dead reckoning is actually pretty easy. Where all of these lines cross is where God probably wants me to be. I think that navigating a relationship with a living God can be just that easy, and the math is easy too. It's Jesus plus nothing.

I used to think following God required complicated formulas. I thought I needed a big stack of books, so I could figure out exactly where I was all the time. I thought if I constantly measured the distance between me and God, I'd get closer to Him. Early on, the religious people I knew explained to me all kinds of nuances for doing this sort of spiritual math. They suggested that I say certain things in my prayers, have quiet times, go to Bible studies, and memorize Bible verses. They said I needed to know how to explain to someone that God could be a person and a spirit at the same time. They urged me to know how God was going to come back someday but that some people would be here and other people would go missing because it would be a time of great tribulation. They said that for me to know God, there was a whole pile of things I'd need to know first. Honestly, they sounded a lot like the guy in aisle three. What I realized, though, is that all I really needed to know when it came down to it was the direction I was pointing and that I was somewhere inside the large circle of God's love and forgiveness.

I've made refinements and countless midcourse corrections in my life. There have been more than a couple of times when I've navigated potentially disastrous issues and needed more exact and specific direction. And when I did, I had the resources I needed to figure it out. But most of the time, even though the guy in aisle three and some religious people would squirm, just pointing in the right general direction has been good enough. I think that's probably because I see myself floating in a massive sea of God's love. The circle of His grace and forgiveness is big enough and the line leading to Him is long enough that I don't need to always be measuring latitude and longitude to find myself. It's a pretty easy calculation each day actually. I'll tell you how I do it. I find Jesus, keep pointing toward Him, and stay somewhere in that circle. That's it. You can keep your sextant and almanacs.

·····◆·····

There's a tradition in the Transpac Race no matter when you finish the race, even if it's two in the morning. When you pull into the Ala Moana Marina in Oahu, there's a guy who announces the name of the boat and every crew member who made the trip. There's a huge loudspeaker, and his booming voice bursts through the trade winds and welcomes each person home. It's the same guy, and he's been announcing each boat's arrival at the end of every Transpac Race for decades.

I'll spare you most of the details of the trip. Just know it involved a lot of water, some stinky dudes, overblown stories of manhood, and lots of canned meats and chili. Just when we came to the end of our supplies, we sailed across the finish line just off Diamond Head and into the marina. It was a few hours before dawn. It had been sixteen days since we set out from Los Angeles in our little boat knowing very little about navigation. Suddenly, the silence was broken by a booming voice over a loudspeaker announcing the name of our tiny boat. Somehow, the way he said it, we sounded like we were the size of an aircraft carrier. Then he started announcing the names of our ragtag crew like he was introducing heads of state. One by one he announced all of our names with obvious pride in his voice, and it became a really emotional moment for each of us onboard.

When he came to my name, he didn't talk about how few navigation skills I had or the zigzag course I'd led us on to get there. He didn't tell everyone I didn't even know which way north was or about all my other mess-ups. Instead, he just welcomed me in from the adventure like a proud father would. When he was done, there was a pause and then in a sincere voice his last words to the entire crew were these: "Friends, it's been a long trip. Welcome home." Because of the way he said it, we all welled up and fought back tears. I wiped my eyes as I reflected in that moment about all the uncertainty that had come with the journey, all the sloppy sailing and how little I knew. But none of that mattered now because we had completed the race.

I've always kind of thought that heaven might be kind of a similar experience. I read somewhere in the Bible that there is a book of life. I don't think that this book of life is full of equations, and I don't think that it's just a list of names either. I think that this book of life is more like a book of lives, a book of stories. I bet it's about people traveling in the direction of Jesus, trying to follow Him. People like me who made lots of mistakes and midcourse corrections. It's about people who stayed within the large circle of His love and grace, staying the course on a long line pointing toward Him. And their names weren't in the book because of what they did or didn't do. They were in there because of who God is and what He has done to draw a circle around them.

After we each cross the finish line in our lives, I imagine it like floating into the Hawaiian marina when our names were announced, one by one. And at the end, perhaps simple words spoken by a loving and proud God will be, "Friends, it's been a long trip. Welcome home."

CHAPTER 24

LOSE THE CAPE

I used to think I should talk about everything,
but now I know it's better to keep some things a secret.

D o you know the movie *The Incredibles*? There's a superhero dad in the movie, and he's tired of his desk job. He sells insurance, I think, but he knows that's not the real him. So he starts doodling on his sketch pad, drawing different superhero suits because he wants to go back to being who he knows he really was meant to be. Most of the outfits he draws have capes because that's how most superheroes dress, and he wants to be the same as them.

He has a friend, Edna, who makes superhero uniforms, and every time he shows her a design, she keeps telling him to lose the cape. She shows him video clips of superheroes who wore capes, and in the end, the capes caused big problems for them, like getting caught on something and causing them to be sucked through a jet engine or worse. That's her reason for my favorite line in the movie: "No capes." Her point, I think, is that you can get a lot more stuff done without a cape. I think Jesus agrees.

It seems like every time Jesus did an incredible thing, He would say something similar to the people nearby. He raised a little girl from the dead, and what did He say? "Tell no one." He met a guy with leprosy and healed him, and said, "Tell no one." He healed two guys who were blind, and He gave them one admonition before moving on: "Say nothing to anyone." In a world driven by self-promotion and spin, Jesus modeled something different for us. Jesus was saying that instead of telling people about what we're doing all the time, there's a better way. One that doesn't require any capes that can get snagged on something—something like ourselves. Maybe Jesus wants us to be secretly incredible instead. That was His plan for self-promotion. Secretly incredible people keep what they do one of God's best-kept secrets because the only one who needs to know, the God of the universe, already knows.

Being secretly incredible goes against the trend that says to do anything incredible you have to buy furniture and a laptop, start an organization, have a mission statement, and labor endlessly over a statement of faith. Secretly incredible people just *do things*. To be sure, mission statements can have a purpose and statements of faith too, I suppose, but are they really necessary? I don't think so. Most times, mission statements are just a catchy sentence or two about how noble the task is, and maybe by implication, how noble we are. The truth is, the task would probably be even nobler if we didn't talk about it and just did it instead.

It's not about being secretive or mysterious or exclusive. It's about doing capers without any capes.

It's usually only religious people who know what a statement of faith is anyway. I guarantee the guy at the deli doesn't. The religious people are the only ones who tease out the missing word or phrase needed to fall in line with their view of faith or doctrine. Their lives aren't really changed by it, of course, and yours isn't either. Getting religious people to agree with detailed mission statements or statements of faith is the same. It's kind of like getting people who already own Chryslers to feel good about owning Chryslers. I'd rather trade all the religious jargon for the chance to invite one person into experiencing Jesus.

You want a mission statement to go along with being secretly incredible? Okay, here it is: "Be Awesome." That's it. If you want to follow Jesus' example of how He did things, that's probably all we'd write down instead of our otherwise heady doctrinal statements. But there's more. I don't think Jesus wants us to make a fashion statement or be edgy or promote ourselves on the backs of clothing and bracelets all the time either. I think instead, Jesus wants us to write "Be Awesome" on an undershirt where it won't be seen, not on the back of a hoodie.

Jesus hardly talked to anyone about what He'd done. The Bible never depicts one of those end-of-camp slideshows where Jesus goes over all He had done with His disciples. Instead, Jesus modeled that we don't need to talk about everything we've done. It's like He was saying, what if we were just to do awesome, incredible stuff together while we're here on earth and the fact that only He knew would be enough? If we did that, we wouldn't get confused about who was really making things happen. Not surprisingly, we'd get a lot more done too, because we wouldn't care who's looking or taking credit. All that energy would be funneled into awesomeness. Even then, though, don't take the bait that if we do incredible things Jesus will dig us more. He can't. He already digs us more. And more than that, our pictures are already in His wallet.

There were two guys named Judas who were among the twelve who followed Jesus. There was the bad Judas, who betrayed Jesus and is the Judas we all know about, and there's also the good Judas, a guy also known as Thaddeus. I hadn't ever heard about him. I can imagine the good Judas telling everyone for the rest of his life, "Just call me Thad." I can also imagine he was probably the first guy to want to go into the witness protection program.

After Jesus left, the ones who were following Him decided they needed to add another apostle to replace the bad Judas. The requirements were pretty straightforward: the replacement needed to have been with Jesus the whole time He was here, and he had to be a stand-up guy too. There were two guys the apostles came up with.

One was a guy named Matthias, and the other guy was nicknamed Justus. I'm not sure how they cast lots back then. Honestly, it sounds a lot like rock, paper, scissors to me. Somehow, however, they picked Matthias. He got the nod and has been in every stained-glass window from then on. But I've always wondered, what happened to Justus? We never hear about him again, yet he did all the right things, saw all the right stuff, knew who Jesus was, and was a faithful guy.

The thing is, "Justus" sounds a lot to me like "just us." God's plans are full of just-us kind of people. I would say probably the majority of us are just-us people, folks who don't get capes or stained-glass windows. We just get the opportunity to do what God wants us to do without a lot of fanfare.

Even though he lost paper, rock, scissors, I bet Justus was one of those secretly incredible guys who kept on being incredible. We get the same shot. Getting passed by can feel like a great injury. But it's not. It's people like us who can be secretly incredible and get the most done. That's the way Jesus' reverse economy works. God loves the humble ones, and the humble ones often don't make it as first-round draft picks for the jobs with big titles or positions. But they always seem to be the first-round picks for God when He's looking for someone to use in a big way. Jesus' message is a simple one. We all get a chance to be awesome if we want to be. Not surprisingly, the way to do it best is by being secretly incredible.

We don't know who lowered a friend through the roof to get him in front of Jesus. We never learn the names of any of the guys who were part of the caper. I wouldn't be surprised, though, if they were people just like us and were wearing undershirts that said "Be Awesome." And I'll bet you one more thing: They weren't wearing capes.

··

CHAPTER 25

GOD IS GOOD

I used to think God was good some of the time,
but now I know He's good all the time.

I had a friend named Don Valencia, and I miss him. Don Valencia was another one of those secretly incredible guys. He was about my age and full of life when we met. He loved to backpack and race cars and climb mountains, and he'd tell stories about sleeping high above the tree line or racing his car for a grueling twenty-four hours nonstop just to see if he could do it. While I'm not a mountain climber and I don't race cars, the more climbing and racing stories Don told me, the more courageous I felt about whatever I was facing.

We all have these friends, these amazing people who seem

to live on the edge of death. It must be because it's on that edge where they feel most alive, where they have the best perspective on life. It's where one missed step, one wrong move would end it all that they realize all over again how beautiful the place they're standing actually is, a place where they live and breathe and love well. Have you noticed that lots of people who trust God seem to be wired to live near the edge?

Don's love for adventure translated into his work as a cell biologist. I'm not sure what a cell biologist does exactly, but I know it has something to do with being really smart. Not afraid of death, early on in his career, Don played with some of the world's most devastating diseases by freeze-drying cells so they could be studied. He would literally freeze-dry death and put it under a microscope. It was like Don had a keychain full of keys to doorways opening up to a better existence, and he spent his life sliding the keys into locks to see if they could be opened. I'm sure Don found it ironic that something so ugly as a disease could be redeemed by God and turned into a doorway leading to joy and freedom and a cure.

One day while preparing for a backpacking trip, Don decided to use his freeze-drying technique on coffee. He loved having a cup of coffee on the side of a mountain but was picky when it came to what he brewed. None of the freeze-dried stuff at the supermarket would do. He tinkered with different beans and different roasts until one day his wife, Heather, stopped by a little start-up coffee shop in Seattle and found some beans she thought her husband might be able to use. She brought the beans home like Jack and his fabled beanstalk. Don freeze-dried them and discovered this new coffee wasn't just good; it was amazing. Don shared his concoction with other backpacking friends and nobody could believe the coffee had been freeze-dried. I think that after they got in the mountains together at altitude and had a cup together, his friends kept looking around to see where the hidden coffee shop was where Don scored the fresh coffee.

That little coffee shop in Seattle Heather found exploded into franchises, so Don decided to share his creation with the CEO, a guy named Howard Schultz of Starbucks fame.

Howard opened the package Don sent him and tried the freeze-dried coffee with, I'm sure, a pack of skepticism. It wasn't long, though, before he jumped on a plane to visit Don in his kitchen. They talked for hours as Don explained the process he'd gone through to preserve the flavor of the coffee beans. Faster than you could lace up a pair of hiking boots, Howard hired Don. No kidding, Don Valencia was suddenly living in Seattle heading the research and development arm of Starbucks. No longer doing his work on the kitchen table, Don now had a multimillion-dollar laboratory for his experiments.

People who take huge risks aren't afraid to fail. In fact, they love to fail. It's because failing means they found the edge. Don created some amazing products for Starbucks, but not all of them worked out. Have you ever heard of Mazagran, for instance? Exactly, me neither. Mazagran was a carbonated coffee-flavored soda that Don invented and Starbucks rolled out quite a few years ago. The only problem was—no one liked it. Don didn't seem fazed with disappointment. In fact, one of the first times I visited Don, I walked up his driveway and saw his license plate that proudly read "Mazagran." The guy celebrated stunning failures like I celebrated my biggest successes.

Don taught countless numbers of people how beautiful it is to fail. More so, he demonstrated how beautiful it is to keep trying nevertheless, to keep moving forward and loving yourself enough to love your mistakes. It was that same spirit of adventure and dedication to redeem failure that led Don to create the science behind a coffee-flavored icy concoction called the Frappuccino. That one ended up doing pretty well.

Don kept perfecting his freeze-dried coffee, sharing it with friends who were backpackers and the inner circles at Starbucks. Everybody loved the stuff, but for decades Starbucks wasn't sure if or how they'd release it. I think they were concerned that freeze-dried coffee might hurt the brand Starbucks had established by serving the freshest, highest-quality brew. Don's delectable freeze-dried crystals got out to a few people, however, so Starbucks had to give the project covert names like "stardust" and "space needle" and even "jaws." If you worked close to Don and were on your way to summit Mount Rainer or had an adventure on the Pacific Crest Trail, you could get your hands on a scarce supply of his concoction. I imagine it looked like a drug deal going down as a nickel bag of "stardust" changed hands and was slipped into a coworker's backpack next to the ice ax and crampons.

Almost two decades later, Don's secret was still under wraps. By that time, Don had retired from Starbucks and had decided to throw himself and his family into different adventures. While always a lover of people, Don had a growing interest in serving them in more tangible ways. He joined the board of a fantastic organization called Agros, which serves the rural poor in Central America, Mexico, and places in the world where the needs are immediate and great. Don moved the family to Central America for a time so they could immerse themselves in both culture and the service. Dwarfing his passion for all of these things, Don found himself closer to God in the adventure of helping people than he ever had been standing on the edge of a cliff.

Not long after returning, while on a trip to Whidbey Island with the Agros board, Don began to feel a terrible pain in his side. He was whisked to the hospital and diagnosed immediately. He had metastasized stage-4 cancer of the liver and lungs. He was now struggling with the same kinds of diseases he'd studied under the microscope for years.

During his brave fight with cancer, Don continued living in a spirit of risk and adventure. It was plain that he was never afraid to die, and he began to chronicle his journey. I'd read his letters and posts along with many other people, and his spirit of love and hope and anticipation was inexplicable. He said he felt like he was dancing on the edge of heaven—but he wasn't scared. He was almost like a commercial telling everybody about how great it was to have cancer. He was that delighted about the opportunity to live even one more day, to take one more breath, to learn one more thing about the character of God. He wanted to move from dancing on the *edge* of heaven to being *in* heaven.

Don lamented, to be sure, that when he stepped into heaven he would be leaving his wife and two sons behind for a time. He fought the disease for them and asked God to let him stick around to make as many memories as possible with the people he loved the most. Each time Don wrote a letter or post, he'd end with these words: "God is good, all the time. God is good." It wasn't just something he was telling himself, hoping it was true. It was something he knew for certain, and he was hoping we'd know too as he stood at the edge of heaven. It was like he was peeking through a knot hole in the fence at the face of God and telling us what he saw on the other side. When Don spoke, you knew without a doubt God was good. And with every letter, it was as if Don somehow picked the lock again and swung the vault door open so we could all look inside at the treasure.

Don hiked his last miles valiantly, beautifully, knowing that death was just a doorway to something better, something we only see traces of in this life. He saw the love of God in his bride and in the joy he found spending time with his sons. He knew the tunes he heard from his perch on the edge of heaven were just faint songs now, like a favorite song he couldn't quite make out but he still knew the words even if his pitch wasn't perfect. You could see in his face that someday he would joyfully join the chorus, maybe as a background vocalist or something.

During our friendship, Don had been up to a lodge we built in British Columbia, and in a season of surprising energy while he fought his cancer, he asked if he and the family could come up to create a family memory. I agreed, of course, and we made plans to receive the man who was teaching so many of us just how good God was. A week before Don and his family were to come, though, his health and energy cratered and Don found himself back in the hospital doing battle with the effects of his advanced disease. Not wanting his family to miss out on a time to recharge at the lodge, Don asked them to make the trip anyway and leave him behind. He wanted them to have a break as they moved into a season where fewer chapters would be written together.

We worked out the details of transportation and communication so we could get the family back to Don in case he needed anything, and the family agreed with Don's wishes to spend a couple of days amid the beauty of the inlet Don had come to love so deeply. It was as though Don was sending the family on an adventure so they could come back and report every detail—what they'd seen and smelled and experienced—and he could live it through them in their stories.

Heather and the boys arrived at the lodge, and while Sweet Maria greeted them, I called Don and we spoke on phone. He was in his hospital bed and we talked about what he was learning about God and how his energy was holding up. Then our conversation turned to the possibility of one last great caper. We laughed about the idea of springing him from the hospital and sneaking him up to the lodge. I felt like I was back in high school plotting to put the principal's car on the roof, and before we realized how absurd it was, we were putting the finishing touches on our caper to get Don to the remote inlet to surprise his family. We hung up the phone believing God was in the caper, and Don instantly had dozens of friends in on it too in order to pull it off. The only ones who didn't know what was being planned were his family. Don figured out how to get the staff to spring him, tubes and all. He was shuttled to a seaplane waiting for him a few miles away in Lake Union and it was game on.

Don was weak, very weak. The plane ride was long. In fact, it was way too long. The seaplane hit fog halfway to the lodge and was grounded for the night. Don took on all the medical procedures that were typically done by a team of nurses. He did them himself in a small bathroom, and he must have felt like he was patching up a wound in the wild bivouacked on the side of a cliff in a snowstorm.

The next morning I was up early listening to the aviation channels in the radio room at the lodge. Then a crackle came through the static from a friend who was the pilot. The plane was just a few inlets away and closing in fast on his family. I asked about how Don was doing and was told he was almost giddy through the tremendous pain and complete exhaustion of the trip. I realized that Don was right back in his zone—on the edge.

I asked Heather and the boys to go down to the dock with my family, explaining that I needed help with a little project and a seaplane would be arriving with some groceries that needed carrying. A short time later, as the seaplane engine stopped and drifted to the end of the dock, I occupied them with a task behind a building so they wouldn't notice the plane's surprise cargo.

Don emerged wearing a red North Face jacket as though making the final ascent on one of the many peaks he'd scaled in his life. Any mountain would have been dwarfed, however, by the one he had just scaled to get to his family. Heather, glancing up from her task, looked once and then again in disbelief. "Don!?" If there were subtitles coming from her mind, they'd probably read: *How is this possible? You're supposed to be in the hospital fighting for your life!*

She exploded to her feet and in three gallops fell into Don's strong arms.

We made our way up to the lodge and Don laid down on the large couch in the living room. The boys sat at his feet and Heather laid by his side. Our family disappeared into the kitchen but could hear them talking softly, then laughing, then talking softly again. They talked about snowboarding and photography and adventures that lay behind and ahead. Heather and Don held hands and looked into each other's eyes a lot, and without getting up from the couch they slow-danced on the edge of heaven together.

Don gave me the gift of a last, meaningful conversation too. I had come to love this man. When the family had left, I laid down on the couch and put my head on his chest. We talked about heaven and eternity and how we would all be back together at some point. And we talked about how God is good all the time, not just some of the time.

Don went to be with Jesus shortly after his last adventure at the lodge, and then Starbucks decided it was time to roll out their best-kept secret. What Don had created twenty years earlier became a reality. VIA, as it's known and seen in every Starbucks around the world, is named after Starbucks's first brave inventor: Don Valencia. Who knows how many backpackers have sat down in the great cathedral of the mountains and shared a cup with a man they've never known but with whom they share the same love of life and risk and beauty? Perhaps those hikers who are looking out over the valleys below, watching the fog roll up the rivers from the ocean, are only suspecting something Don Valencia knows to be absolutely true.

That God is good, all the time. God is good.

....

CHAPTER 26

JAILBREAK

I used to think there were some prisons you couldn't escape,
but now I know there's no place I can go where God can't rescue us.

H ello, I'd like to speak to Attorney General Ashcroft please."
"Who should I say is calling?" the secretary at the other
end of the line asked.

"Bob Goff."

"Bob who?"

I get that a lot.

The secretary told me to call back in two hours, which was
great, because I was late to a lunch meeting with a friend, Charlie.

⋯••◆•••⋯

Charlie had asked me to have coffee with him a week earlier. I'd
known Charlie for a number of years. He's another one of those

secretly incredible guys who doesn't measure his value by what he has but by what he'd be willing to give up. Charlie is a bright guy, had graduated from law school, and spent his life pursuing justice. But all of his accomplishments were like sawdust on a carpenter's floor compared to his desire to love God and express that in what he does.

Charlie said he had something on his mind and I was looking forward to hearing how I could help as I drove to a nearby Starbucks where we decided we'd meet. Charlie beat me there by a few minutes and had already staked out a table in the sun.

"Hi, Charlie, how are you doing?" I said as I walked up.

After talking about our kids and what we thought the next couple months would look like, Charlie shifted in his seat a little and I figured I was going to learn why he had wanted to get together.

"Bob, I've been thinking about this a lot and I've decided that I want to use my legal training to help kids and fight injustice more directly." I nodded in agreement.

I could see in Charlie's eyes a focused determination as he talked about how God loved justice and kids and how much he did as well. We talked about the investigations and raids we had been conducting over the past several years in India and Uganda to help kids get out of brothels and other forms of trafficking. We talked about how I hoped to continue to take the fight to the bad guys by enforcing the laws on the books of the various countries we were working in. Charlie was focused and leaning forward as we spoke, the position of his body taking on the position of his forward leaning heart.

We both lost track of time in our conversation as we talked about how much had been done and how much was left to be done. After a few hours, we pushed back from the table and stood up.

Charlie shot out his hand to me. "Let's do this thing. I'm in," he said.

I laughed to myself because I hadn't proposed anything to Charlie, much less a job. But Charlie didn't make his statement like he was applying for a job. He announced it like he had just created one. Honestly, if anything, I felt like I was applying to work for him.

After pausing for a second and grinning, I shot my hand back.

"Charlie, it's a deal. Do you want to head up all of our investigations for Restore International?"

"You bet," he shot back in an instant.

And with that, we each started walking toward our respective cars. Halfway there, I looked over my shoulder and shouted to Charlie.

"Hey, Charlie, want to know what we pay for the position?"

"Sure," he shouted back across the hoods of three cars.

"Pick a round number!" I said.

"Zero!" Charlie said as he belly laughed and kept walking, shaking his head.

"Hey, one last question," Charlie shouted to me as he got to his car. "What are the benefits?"

"No income taxes!" I yelled back as I got into my Jeep and started the engine.

Charlie quit his job at the FBI and showed up at my office the next day with a couple cardboard boxes full of his things. The larger of the boxes had a plaque from his desk in it. "Agent Walker" is all it said. I can't lie, that registered on my cool meter. Charlie had been with the FBI for years and he was ready to find a new way to serve God and love kids. Charlie moved in over the Laundromat with me, which is where we operate Restore

International. It's not your typical office, but we decided a long time ago that we weren't going to be typical lawyers.

Charlie had served under several attorneys general, including John Ashcroft. I told Charlie about my call to his office and my plan. I told him that I thought I'd tear a page from the kids' playbook and ask General Ashcroft to come with me to Uganda. Why not? I'd seen him on CNN a couple times and I felt like we'd really connected. I was sure he'd felt the same about me.

John Ashcroft is a striking man, full to the brim with both integrity and humility. I knew this when he boasted to me later about being the only man he knew of to ever lose an election to a dead guy. As the former governor of Missouri, he'd spent some time as a senator. His reelection bid failed, however, after his opponent who was the sitting governor tragically died in a plane crash a few days before the election. Too late to be removed from the ballot and in an outpouring of love and respect, the dead politician became the first person posthumously elected to the Senate. Far from done, John Ashcroft was tapped by the president shortly afterward to be the next attorney general for the United States and in that role, headed the FBI through the September 11 tragedy and several other defining moments in our history.

I tried to make contact with General Ashcroft quite a few times. One day, inexplicably, I had the chance to get a message through to him to see if he would come with me to Uganda to make friends with the judges and president. I'm sure he was thinking, *You want me to do what?* Followed by, *Bob who?*

We made arrangements to get together and met a few days later in Washington, DC. The author of the Patriot Act, General Ashcroft was probably more amused than anything else to meet me as I spoke quickly and excitedly to him, waving my arms a lot. "You've just got to come. Everyone will be there. We'll have the president of Uganda there, all the judges, everyone." He asked me to give him all of the other details for the trip. I paused, cocked my head, and looked a little confused. I told him I *had* just given him all the details and started waving my arms around as I explained my idea again. We'd just go and see what happened. That was the plan. In the end, just as inexplicably as we had connected, he said he'd come. A short time later, Agent Walker and I landed in DC, General Ashcroft got on the plane, and we left for Uganda.

I had hired security because of some current tensions, and when we landed in Entebbe we were met on the airport tarmac by at least a dozen guys with machine guns and sunglasses. They circled us and looked foreboding as they struck chiseled poses and looked outward with their backs to us. I felt like I was in an action movie, but for the first time hoped I wouldn't see anything blow up. We left the airport in a motorcade and when we made our first stop to stretch our legs, I asked one of the guys with a machine gun if I could just squeeze off one short burst in a field. He looked at me with one of those *I'm not amused* looks. Maybe later.

In Northern Uganda, because a twenty-plus-year civil war was still raging between the government on one hand and the Lord's Resistance Army on the other, no High Court judge had been to a city like Gulu for more than two decades. What this meant was that justice had been crippled, leaving hundreds of human rights and other cases unheard. I thought we could help. So I had purchased the entire Ugandan law library—both books.

We started briefing those cases that hadn't been heard and began preparing them for trial. We hadn't been asked to brief cases, of course. We just kind of assumed we could. That's one of the things about love. It always assumes it can find a way to express itself.

We asked several brave judges to travel with us to Gulu to start bringing the cases to trial. As inexplicably as John Ashcroft saying he'd come, these judges said they'd come too. Once again, we didn't need to unfold our nonexistent game plan on the table. The game plan was simple. We'd just start doing stuff together—and we did. Lots of it.

After we'd brought over two hundred cases to trial in Gulu, the plan that materialized was to bring together all of Uganda's judges, the president, and General Ashcroft to meet, develop friendships, and talk about what had happened and what was possible. Organizations have programs. People have friends. Friends trump programs every time.

I welcomed everyone to the meeting, introduced General Ashcroft, and we spent the next couple days talking about what Uganda's laws were regarding children and the need for a law prohibiting the trafficking of persons in the country. We also talked about the countless number of young people who had been waiting in Ugandan jails for years without ever having stepped into a courtroom. I wondered what it would be like to be a kid and be put in a Ugandan jail cell. So my friends and I started going to the Ugandan jails that housed the kids to find out.

It wasn't long before we had visited every juvenile jail in the country. Most of them were old and dilapidated concrete buildings surrounded with razor wire on the walls. It was as if all of the buildings were trying to escape, one piece of rust at a time. Inside the typical jail would be one hundred or more young Ugandan boys and a dozen girls aged twelve to seventeen.

Charlie and I went to one of the jails. I asked the warden

what these kids had been charged with. Mostly it was small crimes, petty thefts and the like. However, some were charged with the more serious crime of defilement—having consensual relations with the other sex before eighteen. Unfortunately, what can happen is that the parents of a girl in the village who don't approve of a local boy can simply accuse him of defilement. This alone is enough to land him in jail that day.

Charlie and I looked in the registry that listed the names of each of the inmates and the dates they arrived in the jail. It turned out that most of these young people had been in jail for two or three years. I asked how many of the young people had been to court.

"None," the warden said.

"None? How come?" Charlie asked.

"We don't have enough gas money to get them there."

"You're kidding, right?" Charlie said as he motioned to the court house which we could all see from the warden's office. "Let's just walk there right now."

"It's not as easy as that," the warden answered. "Actually, there are no judges to hear the juvenile cases."

I got Charlie out of the warden's office because Charlie looked like he was about to start throwing furniture around. I lost track of him in the jail for the next hour. When I found him, he was in a cell block with two young men. The older one, Kevin, was telling him what he'd been accused of. Really heavy stuff, I'd learn later. Charlie was sitting on the bottom bunk in a dark cell and holding hands with Kevin, praying for him. Charlie prayed that Jesus would somehow get Kevin out of jail and return him to his life.

Afterward, Charlie told me that he felt kind of bad, thinking perhaps he had placed some false hopes in Kevin's mind by praying for his freedom. Given the gravity of the charges against

Kevin, it seemed a lot more probable that he would spend the rest of his life in jail. Over the next few months, I visited with Kevin quite a few times in that jail cell as we prepared his and other cases for trial. Each time I arrived, Kevin would ask about a kind man named Charlie who held his hands and prayed that he'd be able to return to his life again. Grace works that way. It's a kind word from a gentle person with an impossible prayer. It's a force sometimes transmitted best hand to hand in a dark place.

We organized with the court for the trials to begin and delivered a stack of legal briefs we'd prepared. We got a judge assigned, and a short time later, seventy-two cases were set for trial. The children from the jail arrived; their parents arrived; their accusers arrived; the judge arrived; we arrived. It was game day. There was heaviness in the room as the judge started. The children glanced back over their shoulders at their parents, ashamed.

In a brilliant move, the judge asked the children to leave the court room before the trials began and wait in another room as he spoke to the parents assembled. The judge knew that there was a much bigger issue that needed to be dealt with in the room before the trials began. The judge spoke to the parents and his admonition was simple: "Parents, forgive your children." The judge knew that guilty or not, the children would not be able to move forward in their lives without the forgiveness of their parents. A short time later, he walked into the other room where the children were and said, "Children, your parents have forgiven you." The children were brought back into the courtroom and fell into the arms of their parents. They had received what they needed as much as they needed justice. They had received forgiveness.

By the time we had wrapped up the last of the seventy-two cases brought to trial, we had dropped off seventy kids at their homes with all charges resolved. One of the kids was Kevin. He didn't go back to jail because someone had reached into his darkness and prayed an audacious prayer for him that was answered.

What I've learned the more time I've spent following Jesus is that God delights in answering our impossible prayers. The kind of prayers made in a dark cell by someone holding unwashed hands. Prayers asking for the things we couldn't possibly think could happen for us or someone else. Ones we might even feel a little bad saying, as if it's just asking God for too much. But what I forget is that we're talking to a God who knows that what we need the most is to return to Him, to return to our lives. And like the judge, God knows that we can't fully return until we know we've been forgiven.

God pursues us into whatever dark place we've landed and behind whatever locked door holds us in. He holds our unwashed and dirty hands and models how He wants us to pursue each other. Sometimes that means picking up a phone and asking a stranger to do something that seems crazy at first. He invites us to leave perfectly fine careers like Charlie did, and rather than having us apply for a position, He says our lives are the position. And He says to ordinary people like me and you that instead of closing our eyes and bowing our heads, sometimes God wants us to keep our eyes open for people in need, do something about it, and bow our whole lives to Him instead.

We found another set of jail cells in a different region of Uganda. And another after that and another after that. More kids had their hands held in dark cells by strangers and then had their forgotten cases heard by the courts. And after their trials, those kids were also dropped off at their homes to return to their lives.

We found one particularly horrible jail in the bush that had warehoused more than a dozen kids behind an old wooden door for years. A couple of amazing guys from Pepperdine Law School came over and prepared those cases for trial. Those cases were heard, and when the last kid was dropped off at home after their trial, I had that old wooden door ripped off of its hinges. It now stands in the corner of my office. It's a reminder to me that God searches for us, no matter what dark place we're in or what door we're behind. He hears our impossible, audacious prayers for ourselves and others. And He delights in forgiving us and then answering those prayers by letting us return home to Him. It reminds me that when we take Jesus up on His promises, He doesn't just stand in our lives knocking. He rips our small view of Him and what He can make possible right off the hinges.

I've been back to that last jail a couple times and the warden is still a little bent out of shape that I took his door. He complained to me recently that there wasn't a way to keep kids inside that building now with the door gone. Door or no, God answered an impossible and audacious prayer that each of those kids would be able to return to their life. All it took was for a couple people to show up and get some skin in the game. When they did, the ripples that they made began moving outward in concentric circles that are still washing up on the shores of people's lives and are now changing an entire judicial system.

The last time I saw the warden, he asked for his door again. All of the kids had been released and the cell block stood empty. I looked in the empty cell and then back at the warden and I told him that he didn't need the door because justice had arrived in that dark place and there was no one to keep in. The thing Jesus said about setting captives free actually works, so I haven't given the door back and I told the warden I'm not going to. Sue me.

....

CHAPTER 27

THE STORY

I used to think I needed to record stories,
but now I know I just need to engage them.

My son Adam and I bought a sailboat this fall. Actually, I didn't buy it; Adam did. I just went with him when he did the deal. He'd been saving his money for a while and had just enough for a nice rowboat, paddles optional. He told me one day he'd found an old sailboat on Craigslist that was twenty-seven feet long, and he had enough money for it. "How can you get a twenty-seven-foot boat for the small bag of money you've got?" I asked. "I'm not sure, but if he'll sell it, I want it," Adam shot back.

Adam called the guy, and they agreed on a time for the two

of them to meet on the docks. I tagged along like concerned dads do, knowing that you can't get a whole sailboat for a little more than the price of a nice set of golf clubs. I was going to make it a teachable moment, you know, where the dad intervenes when the guy doesn't have a pink slip, or says the boat belongs to a "friend" who is out of the country, or part of the deal involves the guy living on it with his girlfriend, two dogs, and a llama. I was ready to explain to Adam that sometimes there are scams, and he needs to be on his guard for that kind of thing.

When we arrived, however, we found a really clean-cut guy with a big smile and a warm handshake wearing a plaid shirt and some faded blue jeans. The boat was rough around the edges to be sure, but he was down below tidying up and making sure that all of the life jackets were in order, the lines were coiled, and the radio worked. He offered us a couple of sodas when we arrived and said, "Yeah, this has been a great boat. I've really had fun with it." He started telling us all the places he'd gone with it. It wasn't a sales pitch; it was like he was flipping through the pages of a picture book in his mind introducing us to a really good friend of his. He told us about how he was from the Midwest and he'd always wanted a sailboat, so when he moved to San Diego a number of years ago, it was the first thing he got.

He was a research scientist at Scripps Research Institute, part of the research team working on cures for malaria, HIV/AIDS, deafness, blindness, and cancer. I felt pretty awkward and self-conscious as he described what he did, because all I'd done that day was edge the lawn. This was hardly the guy I imagined selling this boat.

"So why are you selling the boat?" I asked, trying to tease out any underhandedness.

"I just don't have the time anymore," he replied. "It kills me to let her go, but it's just time to move on. What I'd love is to find someone who can add to the legacy of this boat." He looked at Adam as he said this, projecting an emboldening *Are-you-up-for-the-challenge?* vibe.

Adam and I both liked that he said it that way, the part about the legacy.

"Is the price you listed on Craigslist a typo?" Adam blurted. He was tired of the small talk, eager to get the deal underway.

"Nope, that's all I'm asking. It's a great price that will only go to the right person."

Adam stuck out his arm for a handshake and confidently said, "I'll take it!"

The scientist paused for a moment, feigning a deep and skeptical deliberation. Then he cracked his warm smile as he reached for Adam's outstretched hand.

Despite the glow of Adam's pride, we had to acknowledge this wasn't a new boat. In fact, it was almost forty years old. The fiberglass looked like it had been ridden hard and put away wet for several decades. You could tell the adventurous scientist bypassed frills like soap, wax, or rubbing compound. Several of the fasteners that hold the sail to the mast were missing. We pulled up the sails, which I'm sure were once bright white, crisp, and had the feel of white starched tin. Now, however, they hung limp like so many bedsheets from the top of the mast.

The two spinnakers onboard should have been labeled "bad" and "worse." They would have made better rust-stained drop cloths than sails. The teak rails looked like pieces of driftwood with every third screw missing and the running lights didn't work. We started the engine, and it coughed like it had been chain smoking oil for years. Down below, the smell of mold, must, and old gasoline was overwhelming. Through that bouquet I also detected a hint of urine. None of this mattered to Adam. What was important is that it was now his sailboat.

We had to get the boat down the coast to a dock we had behind our house. Adam had never been out on the ocean with a sailboat, which could've been a minor issue. We had a choice. We could either plan the trip or just do the trip. We didn't even talk about the option. We raised the sails, spun the winches because we thought we should, and just started sailing. Anything else we'd figure out along the way.

The trip was uneventful and a number of hours later we were rounding Point Loma and into the calm waters of the San Diego Bay. If nothing else, the boat was brimming with whimsy. Whimsy was the gleam in our eyes; whimsy swelled the sails; whimsy swelled our hearts. That's the way whimsy works. It's a renewable, infinite resource that multiplies.

I've come to understand more about faith as I've understood more about whimsy. What whimsy means to me is a combination of the "do" part of faith along with doing something worth doing. It's whimsy that spreads hope like grass seed in the wind. Whimsy reminds me of the Bible, too, when it talks about stuff being like an aroma. It is not an overpowering one, just something that has the scent of God's love, an unmistakable scent that lingers.

Back at the dock, I asked Adam if he'd thought about a name for his boat. We spend the summers up in Canada and invite people to come and stay for a while to have conversations about how life makes sense to them. Adam's usually off on the side serving, fixing an engine, or riding a motorcycle. He's one of those guys who doesn't steal the spotlight. The summer had been filled with discussions about the story that we're telling with our lives and that we could be living a better story. My friend Don told him that. Turns out that these conversations had left a wonderful watermark in Adam's life.

When I asked Adam what he wanted to name his boat, he sat back in his chair for a long minute looking up and to the left. He fiddled with his jeans some and then said, "I want to name her *The Story*." I realized that Adam saw this tattered sailboat completely different than most people would. Most would see an old jalopy of a sailboat better sunk than sailed. For Adam, though, *The Story* wouldn't be a sailing machine; it would be a story machine. To him it was filled with whimsy, wonder, and adventure even before he untied it from the dock.

Adam knows that I have a project I have been working on for years. It's to write down everything I can remember from my entire life. The first bee sting, the first time I touched knees with someone I liked, the first time I flunked out of a course or got a speeding ticket. I don't keep a journal or a diary, and I'll never just write down facts like what I had for lunch or who I was with or where I was. Instead, what I've been writing down are all of the things I can remember that have shaped me, all of the words or phrases that have pinged me, all of the stories that have happened in my life. All in the hopes that one day, as I flip through those pages, I'll see evidence of Jesus in them.

When Adam told me he wanted to name his boat *The Story*, I wondered out loud with him if he had ever thought of writing down all of his memories as well. What Adam said surprised me again. He thought about it for a second or two and said, "Well, you know, Dad, I've thought about that too. Nothing personal, but I realized that right now, I'm doing the things that other people seem to think of as memories someday. It seems like memories are what older people have when they think back about being my age when they could actually do something about them. So I think what I'll do instead of writing things down now is just do lots of things, and then maybe when I'm done doing cool things, I will write them down later."

I always learn a lot from Adam. I want a boat or a motorcycle or a hot air balloon named *The Story* too. I think we should all get back to building that rocket ship we dreamed of when we thought about what our life would be about. I want to be doing things today, not just flipping through crinkled and yellowed mental pictures of what happened a long time ago. I need my own vehicle to get there, though; we all do. That vehicle will look a little different for everyone. One boat size, one story size, doesn't fit all. We each need to get into something of our own each day, something that will take us to a new place, a place that needs us. Perhaps I'll name my boat *Whimsy* and try to untie it from the dock in my mind at least once a day and take it for a lap. Maybe you will too.

If Adam is right about memories being reserved for folks who don't do anything cool anymore, then I don't want to just collect memories anymore. I've been thinking I'll follow love's lead and find some capers worth doing, ones so saturated with whimsy they have to be rung out like a wet towel to be understood fully. I think I'll also have a dinghy that I tie to the back of my imaginary boat. I was toying with naming it *The End*. But I think I'll name it *Get In* instead, because I used to think I needed to record stories, but now I think I just need to engage them.

....

CHAPTER 28

SKIN IN THE GAME

I used to think I needed to pick sides,
but now I know it's better to pick a fight.

picked a fight with a guy named Dale in the seventh grade. He was huge. He almost blocked the sun when he walked by. I didn't like Dale because he was a bully and beat up the little guys. I'm not sure why he didn't like me. I didn't have good looks or a flock of ladies wanting to be my girlfriends. I suppose if acne fomented anger, back then I had enough to start a war. Maybe Dale didn't like me because I wasn't a little guy and I wasn't going to let him push me or anyone else around. Who knows what bullies think, or if they even think? Bullies are people who use conflict as a means for obtaining power. Some young people grow out of this; others don't and become old bullies.

It was pretty easy to pick a fight with Dale. I told him one day when he was beating up another kid that I wasn't going to let him keep doing it. Seriously, in the middle of the romping, I stepped forward from the small crowd that had gathered and said, "Dale, I'm calling you out." That's junior high–speak for "let's have a fistfight."

He spun around slowly with an evil grin on his face, the kind that hungry giants make in the storybooks. He was delighted to have his next victim step forward so willingly. Like we were finalizing some business transaction, we picked the date and time for the fight. A few days later, we went to the cul-de-sac by the school where they were building track homes. A large throng of kids followed. There weren't many fistfights at my school and this was before talk shows turned violent, so this was big news, almost equal to the yearbooks arriving or a snow day, which in California is a *big deal*.

We started our fight with a lot of pushing and shoving and tough talk. Then we slugged each other for a while and traded headlocks. By the time a teacher came over to break it up, Dale was covered in blood. Nobody realized all of it was mine, so I declared myself the winner and we both got suspended for a couple of days. Here's an important thing to note. If you're going to schedule a fight with a bully and risk getting suspended from school, always pick a fight on a Thursday. That way, you get a long weekend out of the deal.

My parents weren't too thrilled by the whole ordeal. Actually, Mom shook her head and said she was very disappointed in me. Dad pretended to enforce her scolding while winking and giving me air high fives behind her back. (Now that I'm an adult, I totally get this, by the way.) Once I had explained my just cause fighting for the helpless, I talked myself out of being grounded for the weekend. And by Monday, Dale and I were back at school exchanging gunslinger stares as we passed each other in the hallways. I was ready to move on—I had lost enough blood. I guess for people who slug people, guys like Dale and maybe some folks you know, they rarely if ever get anything resolved. It's not about resolution for them. It's about fighting.

That fight with Dale, looking back on it, shows me something about my own hardwiring. I got into and graduated from law school idealistic and ready to help people resolve their disputes. I guess I'm driven by the same need to stand up for the little guy but without using my fists. Jesus talked a lot about disputes, and I am surprised He never said *not* to have them. I suppose that's because He knew disputes would somehow be inevitable. What Jesus commented on, though, is a small list of things worth having a fight about. Jesus also talked about how to resolve disputes. He had been the center of quite a few of them, so He would know. He's still been the subject of countless disputes since He was killed. Even death and resurrection don't solve some things, I guess.

While I didn't think I could resolve disputes as well as Jesus, I figured that I could learn from what He said about them. I liked the part where He said that His followers should just find the person with the least credentials to decide the biggest disputes among them. It sounded crazy to me at first, because I'd want to find the smartest person or the most important person or the most powerful person to resolve a disagreement for me. Jesus thought, however, that the least would bring the most to the table. He said that's how His reverse economy worked. I thought it still might work that way, so I decided to give it a try.

Just out of law school, I figured I had all of the qualifications Jesus talked about for helping people with their fights because I was nobody in particular, I was broke, and I didn't have any power or credentials. So I opened up what I called the Christian Mediation Service. I know, catchy name, right? Honestly, I'm a little embarrassed about it now when I look back. But my heart was in the right place as a brand-new lawyer, and I wanted to use my legal education to make a difference.

The first two Christians who came through the door had a dispute that, in a few minutes it was obvious, ran incredibly deep between them. A few minutes more and I figured out that they really hated each other's guts. It wasn't ordinary hate either—it was the kind they make scary movies about. I met them over and over again, and I tried everything I could think of to get them to bridge the huge fissure that divided them. Their hatred for each other came with an unparalleled passion, a hatred so vile that it took my family getting me an incontinent poodle named Riley as a pet to experience it firsthand.

Through our sessions, I determined that these guys were more interested in inflicting pain on each other through the legal system than actually resolving their disputes. All the talk about resolving conflicts using concepts the Bible talked about—things like love, forgiveness, and self-reflection—were just so many words to these guys. Sure, they had all the Christian phrases. On more than one occasion I even heard them belt out Scripture verses at each other like machine-gun fire. What they lacked was the heart of Jesus, which is the lynchpin to resolving anything. Everything else having failed, I considered inviting them to slug it out like Dale and I had. And that's exactly what I did.

I rented a boxing ring, hired a referee, and got two sets of headgear and gloves. It cost me thirty-five bucks I didn't have, but I was so tired of these guys and their Christianese, I'd take on the winner if they wanted. Heck, I'd take them both on. I called the two guys and gave them the date, time, and place where the boxing ring was and said I'd meet them there and we could settle things once and for all.

When I first started following Jesus I wondered what Christians did when they had disputes. Did they even have disputes anymore? I wasn't sure. After a while, though, I realized that people who loved God had disputes just like everyone else. Some people acted religious about it, and they seemed to get even more religious the bigger the dispute was. The religious people also seemed to carry on their disputes remotely and surrounded the dispute with so many twenty-pound Christian words that it was hard to figure out what they were originally mad about, much less resolve anything. Lots of them had to do with what the religious people thought Christians were supposed to be for or against. What struck me as ironic is that the Bible talked about us being like dust or vapor or like other insignificant things. Yet these folks spoke like they were the ones who had made the mountains when it came to how someone else should act. It wasn't infrequent that one of the religious people would accuse the other person of "backsliding," Christian-speak that basically means the other person doesn't act religious enough. I always thought that was a bad choice of words actually, because it made it sound fun, kind of like ice blocking.

I get why people don't want to go hand-to-hand with the depth of kindness Jesus found common. I get why it's easier to just say what sounds like the right stuff from inside a bunker. The problem is, the Bible said the only weapon any of us really has is love. But it's love like a sword without a handle and because of that, sometimes we'll get cut when we pick it up. It's supposed to be close contact, though. Love always is that way. I don't think Bible verses were meant to be thrown like grenades at each other. They were meant for us to use to point each other toward love and grace and invite us into something much bigger.

All of us want to deal with issues from a safe distance. I know I do. But the stakes couldn't be higher with the small conflicts. If we don't get those right, when its game day for big disputes, we'll still be wrapped around the axle with all of the previous unresolved disagreements. That's what was happening to these two guys.

When the day came for the two guys to resolve things in the boxing ring, I was sitting on the edge of the canvas with my sweats and tennis shoes on. I even put a towel around my neck because I saw it on a *Rocky* movie once. I was looking forward to finally resolving this argument, even if it required stitches. Almost predictably, though, neither of the guys showed up, and I never heard from them again.

I still spend a great deal of my professional life resolving conflicts for others. Some people talk about wanting to resolve their conflicts, but more often, they really have a secret, sometimes subconscious agenda to keep the fight going. The trick is figuring out what's really underneath. Are they all Christianese and just looking to swap big Christian words like knives? Or do they want to model what Jesus said, risk being wronged, and through that, experience just how big God is?

There's a character in the Bible named Joshua. Over and over God told Joshua and his posse to be strong and courageous. God doesn't say in the Bible that we're supposed to man up, or dance around the fire naked and tell manly stories. Instead, we're just supposed to be strong and courageous. That's it. The way I read it, it sounds an awful lot like God is calling us out and telling us to pick a fight.

As Joshua was about to enter the land God promised him, he met an angel with his sword drawn in front of him. Joshua must have had some lawyer in him because he asked the angelic warrior something I would ask: "Whose side are you on?" No doubt, Joshua was hoping that the angelic warrior was for them. That's what I'd hope for. I love the warrior's answer to Joshua's question. It was simple: "Neither. Take off your shoes." The angel wasn't interested in picking sides; he wanted them to pick God. The angel told them to take off their shoes because they were on holy ground, just as we are today. Perhaps God doesn't want us spending our time picking sides or teams and trying on jerseys either. He wants us to pick a fight, and He also wants us to pick Him.

I want to pick a fight because I want someone else's suffering to matter more to me. I want to slug it out where I can make a meaningful difference. God says He wants us to battle injustice, to look out for orphans and widows, to give sacrificially. And anyone who gets distracted with the minutiae of this point or that opinion is tagging out of the real skirmish. God wants us to get some skin in the game and to help make a tangible difference.

I can't make a real need matter to me by listening to the story, visiting the website, collecting information, or wearing the bracelet about it. I need to pick the fight myself, to call it out just like I called Dale out. Then, most important of all, I need to run barefoot toward it. But I want to go barefoot because it's holy ground; I want to be running because time is short and none of us has as much runway as we think we do; and I want it to be a fight because that's where we can make a difference. That's what love does.

Sure, it's easier to pick an opinion than it is to pick a fight. It's also easier to pick an organization or a jersey and identify with a fight than it is to actually go pick one, to commit to it, to call it out and take a swing. Picking a fight isn't neat either. It's messy, it's time consuming, it's painful, and it's costly. It sounds an awful lot like the kind fight Jesus took on for us when He called out death for us and won.

....

CHAPTER 29

MEMORIZING JESUS

I used to think I could learn about Jesus by studying Him,
but now I know Jesus doesn't want stalkers.

Have you ever been stalked? I don't think I have, but I suppose
it would be hard to tell if the stalker was any good. Stalking
is one of those creepy things where once you start talking
about it, you imagine it's happening to you. More people trying
to follow Jesus should think about what stalkers do, but not for
the reasons you might think at first.

I get paid as a lawyer to collect information and memorize
facts, and I've gotten really good at it. What I realized about my
faith is that I was doing just that, collecting information and
memorizing things about God. I collected pictures and gathered

artifacts and bumper stickers about Christianity, and I talked about knowing Jesus like we were best friends, when actually, we really hardly knew each other at all. And I memorized Bible verses and the names of the books of the Bible in order and the sequence of a bunch of events as well as who was there. At some point I had to confess that I was stalking Jesus. I was actually creeping myself out a little and I realized I was probably creeping God out too. So I decided I'd stop.

The first thing I did was quit going to what Christians call a "Bible study." A Bible study sounds like a wholesome thing to go to, and honestly, it is. They can come in as many flavors as there are people leading them. At the ones I went to, I learned a bunch of facts and information about Jesus. We might be studying how a guy named Lazarus was raised from the dead by Jesus. The leader would open up a reference book and say something like, "The word *dead* means in the Greek . . ." And then he'd say, "In the Hebrew the word means . . ." Sometimes he'd get really into it and talk about the difference between the Greek version of *dead* and the Hebrew version. Then he'd ask us a compelling question. Something like, "When was the last time you felt dead?" *Huh?* I asked myself. Honestly, who really needs to hear a definition of *dead*? And what difference did it make? I wanted to talk about how I could do a better job following Jesus, how to practice kindness, and what might be possible to do with my faith before I'm the Greek or the Hebrew version of dead.

This guy's intentions were totally pure, so I don't mean to trash him or anything. Plus, most of the things we studied at the Bible study were true and all, but honestly, it just made me feel like a stalker. Like a creepy guy memorizing facts and information about somebody I barely knew. Whatever it was that I needed, I wasn't finding it because I never wanted to *do* anything with what I had learned. Most Wednesday nights, when I left the Bible study, I found I couldn't remember a single thing we'd talked about either. It was like someone put a big magnet on my hard drive after the Bible study was over. I wondered if something was wrong with me. But then I realized the reason I didn't remember anything was because, in the big scheme of things, it really didn't seem important to me. In other words, it didn't intersect my life; it just bounced up against my life on Wednesdays.

What's up with equating "Bible study" with knowing God anyway? Wouldn't it be a horrible thing if we studied the ones we loved instead of bonding in deeper ways by doing things with them? I'd never want to get married to a girl no matter how much I studied her. I'd rather take her sailing or fishing or eat cotton candy with her on a Ferris wheel. I don't think knowing what her name means in Greek is going to help me love her more. In fact, they have a name for guys who just study things about a person they like but don't do anything about it—they're called bachelors.

So I started getting together with the same guys each week and instead of calling it a Bible study, we call it a "Bible doing." We've been at it for fifteen years now, and I've found there's a big difference between the two. At our Bible doing, we read what God has to say and then focus all of our attention on what we are going to do about it. Just agreeing isn't enough. I can't think of a single time where Jesus asked His friends to just agree with Him.

Sometimes, the reason people try to memorize things is that they don't have another reference point from which to connect with a place or idea or concept. I get that. But the funny thing is, until I've experienced something personally, I usually can't remember it. You'd think that by hearing the same things many times, it would become part of us; but most of us just aren't wired to merely hear things and remember them.

Not long ago I listened to a Taylor Swift song called "Love Story" on a flight all the way from the East Coast to the West Coast. I had the song on repeat on my iPod for some reason and as soon as it finished, it would automatically start once again. It's a happy song. Lots of banjo music at the beginning as I recall. If you want to know how many times I heard that song, divide three minutes and fifty-five seconds by North America. Even though I heard the words sung over and over, you know what? I can't remember more than a few isolated lyrics.

I remember that it's about a guy named Romeo and I'm not quite sure who the girl is. I'm guessing it's Taylor. I think that they had to overcome some adversity because the girl's dad wasn't keen on young Romeo. As a dad, I can respect that. But at the end of the day, I can't remember how the song ends or whether the guy got the girl.

I don't remember much about Taylor's love story even though I've heard the song about it over a hundred times. Why, in contrast, can we remember every nuance, every glance, and if we've fallen in love, our entire courtship story with such punishing detail? With our own love stories, every detail comes alive. Our own love stories are so poignant, so detailed, so unforgettable— at least to us. When it's someone else's love story, however, we will be polite and listen, but usually it's entirely forgettable. It's like looking at someone else's vacation pictures.

When I have skin in the game, the outcome all of a sudden matters to me and I become engaged. Some people think of engagement as the time between proposing marriage to someone and getting married. I think of engagement as the time between hearing a truth and nodding our heads or making sincere *mm-hms* in agreement and when we do something about it. That explains why Jesus never talked about just building consensus; He wanted us to build a kingdom instead.

If you get engaged like that, you'll be able to remember Bible verses better because you're *living* them instead of just reading them. Another by-product of engagement is all the canned answers we have to complex questions melt away. I think that's because we see ourselves in the context of something larger that is unfolding. The details aren't distractions; they are ladder rungs we can pull ourselves up on. We remember because we are no longer observers. I think Jesus had in mind that we would not just be "believers" but "participants." Not because it's hip, but because it's more accurate, more fitting that way. He wanted people who got to the "do" part of faith, not because He wanted activity, but because He wanted our faith to matter to us.

One of the ways I make things matter to me is to move from merely learning about something to finding a way to engage it on my own terms. For example, if someone asks what I think about capital punishment, instead of reciting the party line and parroting someone else's thoughts, I think of a teenager named Kevin in a prison in Uganda who had been accused of a capital crime. If the topic is same-sex attraction, I think of a dear friend of mine who is gay. Now instead of talking about an issue, I'm talking about a person, someone who matters to me. I think that Jesus wired us that way so that we'd remember. And it's not about just being politically correct; it's about being actually correct. We need to make our faith our very own love story.

What I like about Jesus' message is that we don't need to study Him anymore to know Him. That's what the religious people at the time were promoting. Collecting information about someone is not the same as knowing a person. Stalkers are ordinary people who study from afar the people they're too afraid to really know. Jesus said that unless you know Him like a child you'll never really know Him at all. Kids don't care about facts, and they certainly don't study each other. They're just with each other; they do stuff together. That's what Jesus had in mind.

I listened to Taylor Swift's song a few more times since my trip across the country. This time I took notes so I'd remember how the story goes. It turns out that it all worked out great in the end for Taylor. Romeo stuck around even though the dad told him to split, she got a white dress, and according to Taylor, all she had to say was yes. But I bet Romeo didn't get to know her because he memorized her. I think it's because he did things with her. It's the same for us.

....

CHAPTER 30

PALMS UP

I used to think clinched fists would help me fight better,
but now I know they make me weaker.

'm not a writer; I'm a lawyer. I think of myself as a recovering lawyer, actually. I sue companies that make crooked skyscrapers or bent buildings. I chose that kind of lawyering because I didn't want to defend a crook or somebody who kicked a dog or ran over their mother-in-law with a golf cart. Don't get me wrong, I'm no softy; I can be extremely confrontational when it comes to dirt and two-by-fours.

Some time ago I stopped thinking about being a lawyer as a career. Instead, I think of it as just a day job. Thinking about work as a day job has made a big difference in the way I approach what I do. It's also helped me not to confuse who I am with what I do.

I spend a great deal of time working for kids in Uganda and India and chasing bad guys who hurt them. I started a nonprofit a number of years ago and now Sweet Maria and I think about my day job as a great way to fund the things we're doing. Now when I put on a suit and tie or jump on a plane to go take a deposition, we call it "fund-raising." It still makes me grin every time to say it this way. It's like a really successful bake sale to get rid of bad guys.

Depositions are my favorite part of practicing law because they involve a lot of strategy. A deposition in a lawsuit is when the lawyers ask people lots of questions. Sometimes I even videotape the deposition, particularly if the person answering my questions has a short temper or a tendency to make things up. People who are like this can turn red and light up like a tomato, and when they do, it makes for a great Kodak moment.

Sometimes my clients have to be deposed, which means they are the ones asked questions by the other guys' lawyers. It can feel intimidating with a big room full of lawyers all staring at you. So when my clients are being deposed, I tell them all the same thing each time: sit in the chair and answer the questions, but do it with your hands palms up the *whole time*. I tell them to literally have the backs of their hands on their knees and their palms toward the bottom of the table.

I'm very serious about this. In fact, I threaten to kick them in the shins if I look down and they don't have their palms up. When their palms are up, they have an easier time being calm, honest, and accurate. And this is important, because it's harder for them to get defensive. When people get angry or defensive they tend to make mistakes. But nobody can be defensive with their palms up.

Go ahead and try it. Right now, wherever you are. Set your hands on your knees and turn your palms toward the sky.

You can try the opposite too. Clinch your fists. Most people could get angry at a grapefruit when their fists are clinched. Something about the hardwiring that God gave each of us links the position of our bodies and position of our hearts. I'm not sure why we're wired this way, but I rarely have a client get frustrated or confused or get tempted to exaggerate or tell a lie when his palms are up.

I learned this technique from Jesus actually. I used to walk around with my fists clinched, defensive, afraid people were going to take advantage of me. There are also many evils in the world that caused me to clinch my fists. I wanted to be angry and swing at the horrible things people do to one another, especially the things done to kids. But it was Jesus who taught me there was nothing I could really lose if I had Him. He taught me to be palms up, just like He was. Palms up means you have nothing to hide and nothing to gain or lose. Palms up means you are strong enough to be vulnerable, even with your enemies. Even when you have been tremendously wronged. Jesus was palms up, to the end.

When people ask me what it looks like to follow Jesus, I usually say that following Him looks like dealing with all of the issues everyone else does—disappointments, tremendous joy, uncertainty, the whole bit—and having your mind change all the time as you learn how Jesus would've dealt with things. Following Jesus is about having your paradigms shift as you navigate a wide range of emotions while living the big life Jesus invites us into. Because I know Jesus, where I once thought of things in one way, now I think of them in another way. It happens all the time, every day.

Jesus seemed to say that a lot Himself. He would say, "You once thought this, but now I tell you that it's different." And through the many paradigm shifts I've had following Jesus, the one that seems to universally apply is that we should be palms up.

....

CHAPTER 31

TWO BUNK JOHN

I used to think that taking a risk would reduce
the number of friends I have,
but now I know that love draws more people in.

've been teaching Business Law at a local university for over
a decade. One year, there was a guy in the third row named
John. He could have been a forward for the Lakers at six feet six
inches tall. He originally planned to be a doctor, then a biologist,
but somehow ended up in the business school at the university
and signed up for my class. Half the time I would be flying in
from Seattle to San Diego to teach, so no one was allowed to be
late to class. I figured if I could travel over a thousand miles and
get to class on time, my students could walk one hundred yards
and make it. John usually just made it by a hair.

It was John's senior year and he was trying to decide what he'd do after he graduated. One day, he invited me over to his house where he and some other graduating seniors got together on Friday evenings with younger guys at the university to talk about how to live a different kind of life—one that wasn't typical. John was a bright and talented guy with an easy personality and a quick smile. He didn't love people the way that Hallmark says to love people; he loved them linebacker style, in a full contact way. You wouldn't even know you'd been tackled by John's engaging love until you walked away, almost sore from it.

I liked that these guys were talking about going off road with their lives rather than arriving at safe places on the map, places that seemed typical to them. I don't think anyone aims to be typical, really. Most people even vow to themselves some time in high school or college not to be typical. But still, they just kind of loop back to it somehow. Like the circular rails of a train at an amusement park, the scripts we know offer a brand of security, of predictability, of safety for us. But the problem is, they only take us where we've already been. They loop us back to places where everyone can easily go, not necessarily where we were made to go. Living a different kind of life takes some guts and grit and a new way of seeing things. John and his friends sounded like they wanted to take their faith off-roading a little, so when John invited me to come and be with his group, I told him I'd be there.

Friday night came and we had a big talk around a small fire. We talked about how we didn't need to operate on the same economy that everyone else did. How we didn't need to do things the way everyone else was doing them. And how we could aim for a life of engagement instead. We wouldn't need a flag or a banner or matching T-shirts or hoodies or even business cards.

We could just do life like a pickup basketball game. If you've got a hook shot, you bring that. If you're not a good shooter, you pass the ball. What's distinctive about this way of doing life is that there are no score keepers or mascots. You just bring all the game you've got. Not surprisingly, the game you've got always seems to be enough.

As the evening wound down, I stirred the coals in the fire a little and hoped I was stirring something inside each of these guys. I could tell I was for John. I told him there was no card trick involved. When you decide to drop everything that's typical, all that is left is just a big idea about an even bigger God and a world that's worn out from the way everyone else has been doing it. The world has been shouting over the noise of our programs that it doesn't need more presidents or organizations, what it needs are more friends. If you are a sincere friend, folks around you will quickly understand that there's no hidden agenda and nothing on the other side of the equals sign—just you.

At the end of the evening, I finished by saying this: "John, I dare you to spin the globe, throw your finger down, and pick a place to plug in. If you don't have another place you'd rather go, why not Uganda?" The strategy we discussed was simple: we'd go make friends and see what happened. Not the typical version of friendship that is often called networking. Instead, we'd be real friends. John would tell me later that this all struck a chord inside of him. Not like a violin, more like a rock band. John was a guy who I could see didn't want to just think about this idea, he was ready to launch off the stage and go crowd surfing with it.

Since we weren't angling to do things the way they are usually done, there wasn't much to discuss either. Like the disciples, we had no plan, no program, and no preparation. I told John I had a whole fleet of airplanes to take him overseas. They all had Delta Airlines written on their sides and for fifteen hundred bucks he could get on one. A short time later, John ducked his head to clear the doorway of a 767 heading for Uganda.

Just because we weren't going to plan everything didn't mean we weren't going to be strategic. It meant just the opposite. Instead of getting wrapped around the axle developing a plan, we used our time to develop a strategy and we had started in Uganda on purpose. It's a country that had been ravaged by a twenty-plus-year civil war leaving millions of people displaced from their villages as virtual refugees in their own country. AIDS and other diseases had wiped out what the war didn't, and an entire generation of Ugandans were simply gone. The population in Uganda at the time had an average age of just over fourteen and a half years old. Uganda had become a nation of children.

When we first began doing our work in Uganda five years before I met John, the country showed the signs of a nation at war with itself. Driving to Northern Uganda in a small car like the one we had wasn't common—UN bullet proof vehicles were the norm. I envied the UN guys and their cars, not just because they looked manlier, but because you wouldn't die. Crossing the Nile River that divided the war torn North from the South during the height of the insurgency, we came across check points and roving military squads carrying machine guns every several miles. It was more than a little creepy. We quickly learned not to stop for anyone in camouflage no matter how emphatically they waved. This is because the insurgents and the Ugandan military wore the same uniforms. We drove as fast as our small car would take us to Gulu where there were military barracks nearby and a little more security. Although Gulu only covers six square blocks, it's the second largest city in the country because most of the population in Uganda lives in the bush.

The entire country had suffered in the war, but Gulu and the surrounding areas in the North had been hammered the worst by the Lord's Resistance Army, led by Joseph Kony, who launched attacks throughout Northern Uganda. His strategy for growing his army was simple: abduct tens of thousands of children. The young boys were given machine guns and put out in front of the older soldiers in the fire fights. The young girls were forced to be child brides. Most of these children were twelve to fourteen years old. What occurred with them was unthinkable. When abducted, the children were often made to kill one or more family members in order to alienate them from the villages and shame them so they wouldn't try to return from the bush. Those who did try to escape were caught and killed in horrific manners as warnings to the others.

Just outside Gulu, we found thousands of kids living in camps set up by the government with no opportunity for an education at all, so we decided to start a school just north of the city. The local officials laid out for us at least three years of hoops to jump through before we could start. This seemed like lunacy to us with an entire generation of kids living in camps without any schools at all and the Lord's Resistance Army still conducting evening raids to abduct more children. We tried to reason with the government officials for a while about waiving the restrictions, and when it was apparent we weren't going to get their cooperation, we decided to open the school anyway.

For the next month or two, we got word out as broadly as we could to the half million displaced people in the region that we were starting a school. It would be called the Restore Leadership Academy. We let everyone know what a great idea this school was and braced for a huge turnout as a result of all of our efforts. On the first day of class, we had a total of four kids show up. But we weren't discouraged at all. We were too busy chest bumping and high-fiving each other. We had a school. It wasn't Harvard—it was better. It belonged to four kids and us.

John's task was to pull together the best Ugandan teachers from the North, assemble a student body, and start. We soon felt oversized and a little awkward with more teachers than students. Suspicions were high among the locals about this small school in the bush with a giant of a man named John running it. It wasn't long, however, before we had twice as many students. We were up to eight. This was explosive growth by our measuring stick. More students found their way to the classrooms, and by the end of the first year we had nineteen, so we started a soccer team. Why not? We had more than enough players. The kids didn't have shoes and the soccer field had a pole and mango tree in the middle it, but our kids never complained. Instead, they told us it gave them a home field advantage.

Soon, there were one hundred kids in the classrooms that were now bulging. And the kids still kept coming. John called me with the great news about the school's growth and stories about students who once carried machine guns and navigated mine fields who were now on the soccer field navigating a mango tree and pole. John told me about two kids in particular who were walking eight miles each day to attend classes and what he thought they needed. It went something like this:

"Bob, would it be possible for us to give these two great kids a place to stay overnight at the school?"

"Absolutely not, John. We're not a boarding school," I responded immediately.

John's thinking was kind and caring, of course, but I remembered that Oprah had started a school in South Africa and run into a pack of trouble arising out of boarding kids and I resolved never to take on that responsibility. Besides, we could barely afford the school and the teachers, much less monitor, house, clothe, and start feeding boarding students.

"Sorry, John, no," I repeated.

"But, Bob, come on. We just need two bunks. That's all, just two bunks," John insisted.

"No, John." I was on my feet signing in the air with my left hand as I was shaking my head vigorously.

"But it's for the kids," John pled.

He was relentless.

I could tell I wasn't going to win this round and John did some Jedi thing I suppose, as I heard myself saying, "All right, John, two bunks for these two kids, but that's it. Just two bunks."

"I promise" were the last words he spoke to me about the bunk beds.

It's now three years later and at last count, we have over 250 full-time boarding kids at the Restore Academy. "Two Bunk John," as we now call him, spends most of his days conspiring with everyone he meets about ways to make these kids' lives richer, more meaningful, and more intentional.

Do you know why all of this happened? It's simple. Two Bunk John got off the map. He wasn't limited by the contours of convention any longer. Instead, he leaked what he loved. He was leaking Jesus. And pretty soon the puddle he made swallowed us all by the lake it formed. That's the way the chemistry of God's love and our creativity work together when combined. No reservoir can hold it, no disappointment can stop it, and no impediment can contain it. It can't be waved off, put off, or shut down. It doesn't take no for an answer. Instead it assumes yes is the answer even when it sounds an awful lot like a no to everyone else.

There's a national test given each year to high school students in the Republic of Uganda. It covers thirteen subjects including algebra, chemistry, physics, history, and geography to name just a few. It's tougher than any test I've ever taken, and John and I wondered just how many of the original nineteen students who had grown up in the bush could pass it. Maybe one? Perhaps two? Some of these kids had been carrying machine guns or leading families when their parents were lost to the war or died of AIDS. None of them had been in school. Honestly, in my mind, this national exam seemed an insurmountable obstacle to these kids continuing with their education. What I had underestimated, though, was the resolve of Two Bunk and the teachers at the Academy.

Shortly after the exams were graded by the national examiners I got a call from John.

"Bob, I'm holding the test results." There was a mean pause that lasted way too long. "Nineteen of nineteen passed!"

We all welled up with tears of joy and pride for what these kids had accomplished. That's one of the things about love. It doesn't recognize boundaries and never obeys the rules we try to give it. It seemed that no one had told Two Bunk or the teachers that they couldn't change the trajectory of the kids' educational futures, and no one apparently told these kids that they all weren't supposed to pass the national exam.

I guess no one told the Restore Academy Soccer team that it was too small, too remote, too underfunded, or too barefoot when it came to playing soccer either. The next year they beat every team in Northern Uganda and boarded a bus headed to the capital to play for Uganda's national soccer title. And no one told one of the Restore girls that she couldn't become Uganda's national top-ranked javelin thrower. Because she did. I didn't even know we had a javelin. I wondered if it was perhaps the pole by the mango tree she was throwing.

The following year, thirty more graduates would all pass the national exam; as did the next thirty-five graduates the year after them. And no one told the entire student body at the Restore Academy when the test results came in this year that they couldn't get the highest test scores in all of Northern Uganda. Because they did.

John and I met out in the bush with the village elders last year and we pointed together toward forty acres of gently sloping African tundra that we had just purchased. We had outgrown the school and ran out of surrounding buildings to rent. It was time to build our own school. None of us thought when we were sitting in John's backyard around a small fire four years earlier that we'd be building an entire village-sized school for more than three hundred teachers and students. We weren't thinking at that time about where the chain reaction would stop, and we're still not thinking about it. I'd like to think it's because we didn't have a plan. We had a big idea instead. You see, the problem with my plans is that they usually work. And if they don't seem to be working, I force them to work and I get the small results I aimed for. Swapping that for a big idea means I get everything that everyone brings to the pickup basketball game. Guys like John, people like you, and everyone else who have joined us.

Just like Two Bunk, we're asking these kids to ignore what's typical too. We want them to be leaders through action, not just in name. Sponsorship programs are common in developing countries. For thirty dollars or so each month, it is not unusual for a child to have a sponsor in the United States to help with school fees. We got the kids together and explained to them how *our* sponsorship program was going to work. We gave our kids some seeds, they planted the seeds, they raised the crops, they sold the crops, and with the money, our kids from the Restore Leadership Academy in Uganda sponsor a little skater kid in Oregon through The Mentoring Project, a fantastic organization out of Oregon that helps kids without dads.

These Ugandan kids looked through the other end of the telescope and wanted to make sure that other kids could have the same input from mentors that they are getting. If these kids in Uganda had a refrigerator, they would have a picture of the kid with a swoop haircut they are sponsoring in the United States on it. That's leadership.

And the chain reaction continues to grow without people even knowing about it. I'll give you one last example. You probably didn't know when you bought this book that everyone—Thomas Nelson, me, my friend Don, everyone—gave all of the money away to launch more kids toward an atypical life. What that means is that now you're part of this fantastic caper too. Because, if I've learned one thing from Two Bunk John, it's that love does whatever it takes to multiply itself and somehow along the way everyone becomes a part of it. You know why? Because that's what love does.

EPILOGUE

You've read the stories in this book, but what's better than all of those stories are the ones you're continuing to write with your life. If you're like me, I'd ask myself at the end of a book called *Love Does—so what do I do?* It can be a tough question to answer, honestly, but it can also be an easy one. Let me tell you what I do when I don't know what to do to move my dreams down the road. I usually just try to figure out what the next step is and then do that. I know it sounds too simple, too formulaic; it seems like there must be more to it. But there isn't. For most of us, that next step is as easy as picking up the phone, sending an e-mail, writing a letter, buying a plane ticket, or just showing up. After that, things start happening. Things that perhaps have God's fingerprints on them. You'll know which ones do and which ones don't. Pick the ones that do.

What's your next step? I don't know for sure, because for everyone it's different, but I bet it involves choosing something that already lights you up. Something you already think is beautiful or lasting and meaningful. Pick something you aren't just able to do; instead, pick something you feel like you were made to do and then do lots of that. You weren't just an incredible idea that God never got around to making. The next step happened for the world when God dropped you on the planet. You're here and I'm here. God decided to have us intersect history, not at just any time, but at this time. He made us to be good at a few things and bad at a couple others. He made us to love some things and not like others. Most of all, He made us to dream. We were meant to dream a lot. We're not just a cosmic biology experiment that ended up working. We're part of God's much bigger plan for the whole world. Just like God's Son arrived here, so did you. And after Jesus arrived, God whispered to all of humanity . . . "It's your move." Heaven's been leaning over the rails in the same way ever since you got here, waiting to see what you'll do with your life.

A couple of the people you met in this book ended up making their next moves. Randy, the guy who taught me about what being with people is all about in Yosemite, now lives with his wife, Sandy, in Nevada and is still changing people's lives with his organization, Doable Evangelism. Not long after he took a knee and proposed, Ryan married Kim and they now have two beautiful children and lead worship at a fantastic church in Orange County.

Two kids from one of those dark jail cell blocks ended up attending the Restore Leadership Academy. The first one of them graduated at the top of his class and the other has a reputation for being one of the friendliest kids on campus. I took the Chief Justice of Uganda's Supreme Court to my office on Tom Sawyer's Island at Disneyland and we dreamed about justice issues in Uganda. And after almost five years in Uganda, Two Bunk John applied to law school and plans to start next year. He won't be sitting on any dean's bench trying to get in; the schools will be fighting over him.

Kathy has lead an amazing life devoted to her family, the cause of injustice, and the abolition of modern-day slavery. Lehr's Greenhouse Restaurant is out of business and I'm still looking for my red jeep. Richard and Adam each have BB guns and go out into the woods together; but they say they never shoot at each other. Yeah, right.

Since high tea in London, Lindsey has become that lovely woman I saw across the table when she was ten. Everyone in the family continues to stay connected with people in leadership around the world, and Don Miller, who taught me not to write the word *that* into my life, made a movie called *Blue Like Jazz* with a friend, Steve Taylor. Through his movie and books, including *A Million Miles in a Thousand Years*, and his Storyline Conferences, Don is continuing to show us how much room there is in the margins of our lives to scribble some notes.

I'm still practicing law and trying to live palms up. I hardly ever go sailing, but I travel to Uganda often to look for kids forgotten in jails and for bad guys who would hurt them. This year, we successfully brought to trial Uganda's first case for trafficking in people against a witchdoctor—and won.

One last thing. I didn't tell Doug I'd be writing a book and telling stories about him. I thought it would be a better prank if he heard it first from you.

ACKNOWLEDGMENTS

It takes a big cast to support the stories that make up this book. It's like a festival of friends, actually. Because of that, this book isn't written by or about the lives of just a few people; it's written and influenced by the lives of many people, whether their names appear in these chapters or not. To each of you who have helped shape the stories and the process of getting them down on paper, I want to thank you. I see evidence of you everywhere in these pages and, more importantly, in my life. Your kindness and encouragement to me has shaped how I see Jesus. It would take a second volume of this book to contain the names of everyone who had a hand in encouraging me, but you know who you are because I've had the privilege of telling most of you in person.

Thank you, Sweet Maria, Lindsey, Richard, Adam, Miss Ashley, and Brad, for being patient with me while I sat in my favorite chair for a year working on this project. The reason it's my favorite chair isn't because it's soft; it's because it's near where all of you are.

Don Miller, none of this would have happened without your friendship, encouragement, and input. You've added more than just words to a book, you added yourself to my life. The same is true of my dear friends Al Andrews and Brandon Heath. The two of you not only show me how good God really is, but you are the kind of guys who make me want to do something about it.

The family of friends who are part of Restore International and share in our work in Uganda and India have become like a big pile of presents to me. Every time one of you is opened up, I dig through the wrapping paper and find three more of you in the pile. That's what happens when you stop acting like an organization and decide to act like a family.

To each of the students at the Restore Academy, we're so proud of you. John Niemeyer, your encouragement and leadership guiding Restore's efforts in Uganda have been nothing less than stunning. Thanks, Ilea Dorsey Angaza, for pioneering the way. Deborah Erikson and the whole Restore International Team living in Uganda, your love for kids floors me. I want whatever you've been eating for lunch. Trent Walters, your style of servant leadership redefines the words *servant* and *leadership* for me. Special thanks to Blake Gaskill and the construction team, as well as Gregg, Karen, Heather, Jim and Julie, Ryan and Crystal, Todd Nelson and his family, George and Bernie, Michael and Marybeth, and countless volunteers who started out serving me and ended up pouring their lives into an entire country. And to the hundreds of people who have engaged the Restore kids and teachers at the Restore Academy—Wow. Look what you've done!

Reggie Whitten, Noah Roberts, Jim Priest, and the entire Pros For Africa Team: you didn't just start with nothing, you started with a nun, Sister Rosemary, and together you've changed much in Northern Uganda and beyond. Chris Cotner, Dick Greenley, and the Water 4 team, the same goes for you. Wells aren't the only things that run deep in your lives. The amazing work being done by the Kwagala project under Kristen's contagious leadership and the people from Invisible Children have encouraged me daily. You've each been amazing friends and encouragers in the process of getting these thoughts on paper, and you are part of every page. These organizations embrace kids in Uganda the way God embraces us and are worth getting involved with.

I'm thankful for the guys in my "Bible doing" too. Steve, Mike, Bud, Jim, Bill, Mike, Jon, and George: you're the guys who helped me stop stalking Jesus and start following Him instead. The same is true of the guys in the 199 Club: Jim, Michael, Don, and Steve. You've given me tremendous strength and encouragement by the courageous way you dive into other people's lives. If I grow up, I hope to be like you. Thanks also to the community of friends in Nashville for making me feel so welcome.

The chance to write this book as well as live the stories in it would never have happened without the efforts of the best law firm in the Pacific Northwest. Danny DeWalt, you are an amazing lawyer, pastor, leader, and friend. Ken, John, Cynthia, Aaron, and Eric, thank you for freeing me up to write this book. The highlight of every year is taking a knee, proposing to you one at a time, and asking if you'll practice law with me for one more year. Thanks for saying yes.

I've found coconspirators in the staff and students at Pepperdine Law School as well. I want to thank Jim Gash, Tim Perrin, and Jay Milbrandt in particular. You've helped me understand just how much God loves justice. My thanks to the students and staff at Point Loma Nazarene University too. I went to teach and serve at both universities, but I ended up being the one who was taught and served. The same goes for Dave Batstone and the amazing team at Not-For-Sale.

ACKNOWLEDGMENTS

I can imagine more because these people are in my life: my parents, Rick and Marti, Doug and Debbie, Rob and Leslie, Harold and Terri and Sharon, and all the friends from Young Life in the United States and Malibu Club, Canada. To the posse of friends who have walked through waterfalls with me at the Lodge, you continue to inspire me as you leak Jesus on a parched world. Tara and Eric, you make it all happen every year and I want to thank you for knitting us together. To the Coes, the Burleighs and Darla Anderson: when I think of each of you, I think of joy, courage, and pure kindness. I've also been surrounded by an incredible community of leaders who spend their days conspiring about how to point people toward Jesus.

Finally, I want to thank the incredible team at Thomas Nelson who have provided outstanding support to me. Bryan Norman, your fingerprints are on every dog-eared page of this manuscript. Brian Hampton, Heather Skelton, Jason Jones, Kristi Henson, Katherine Rowley, and copy editor Jennifer Stair, you should each be wearing capes, but I know you're too humble to. Mike and Gail Hyatt, you are responsible for launching this grand caper. The two of you are who Maria and I want to grow up to be some day.

One last thank you. Chuck and Laurie Driscoll, I understand more about the kindness of God because I live next door to you.

All of the proceeds from the book are being donated to Restore International's Leadership Academy in Gulu, Uganda (www.restoreinternational.org) and the Mentoring Project (www.thementoringproject.org). These two organizations are committed to loving kids in tangible ways and moving the needle in their lives. They're worth getting involved in.

ABOUT THE AUTHOR

ob Goff is the founder and CEO of Restore International, a nonprofit organization fighting injustices committed against children. Restore's mission is to make a difference on behalf of those who do not otherwise have a voice.

Restore International has worked with Uganda's judiciary in more than two hundred cases to free children from wrongful imprisonment without trial. In 2007, the Restore Academy was started, a school in the war-torn region of Gulu, with a current enrollment of 220 students. In India, Restore has intervened to relieve minor girls from a life of forced prostitution, leading to the identification and arrest of over fifty perpetrators.

Bob shares leadership in a Washington law firm, Goff & DeWalt, and is admitted to practice in California and in Washington. He serves as the Honorary Consul for the Republic of Uganda to the United States and is an adjunct professor at Pepperdine Law School (Malibu) and Point Loma Nazarene University (San Diego).

CONNECT WITH BOB

One of the things I've learned following Jesus is how much He enjoyed being with people. Except for time with His Father, there seemed to be nothing He loved more. He didn't just love the *idea* of being with people either, He actually loved being with them. A lot of people in the world stop being available at some point. It's subtle, because it happens a little at a time and it's not malicious or anything—it happens though. But Jesus wasn't that way. He seemed to have more time for people as time went on, not less. That's one of the things which makes love so powerful; it leaves us a way to find it.

The same thing is true about people who have shaped my world view. I've found that the people in my life who have actually been the most influential have also been the ones who were the most available. If you ever want to talk about any of the ideas in this book that ping you, my phone number is (619) 985-4747. Give me a call sometime if I can be helpful.

DISCUSSION QUESTIONS

Thinking of going deeper? Chapter by chapter questions are available for your personal or small group use. Download the pdf at these websites:

nelsonfree.com/LoveDoes
bobgoff.com/lovedoes